MLA HANDBOOK

FOR WRITERS OF RESEARCH PAPERS, THESES, AND DISSERTATIONS

STUDENT EDITION

JOSEPH GIBALDI
WALTER S. ACHTERT

MODERN LANGUAGE ASSOCIATION   NEW YORK   1980

© 1977 by The Modern Language Association of America
Library of Congress Catalog Card No. 77-76954

ISBN 0-87352-000-9 (student edition)
0-87352-450-0 (reference edition)

First edition

First printing, 250,000 copies (student edition), August 1977
Second printing, 150,000 copies (student edition), August 1978
Third printing, 30,000 copies (reference edition), October 1979
Fourth printing, 200,000 copies (student edition), July 1980

MLA HANDBOOK

FOR WRITERS OF RESEARCH PAPERS,
THESES, AND DISSERTATIONS

CONTENTS

ACKNOWLEDGMENTS

Based on William Riley Parker's *The MLA Style Sheet* (1951), as revised in 1970 by John H. Fisher and others, the *MLA Handbook for Writers of Research Papers, Theses, and Dissertations* reflects the thinking and incorporates the suggestions of teachers, scholars, and students throughout the United States and Canada.

Although it would be impossible to acknowledge everyone who assisted us with this project, we would like to express our gratitude to a number of persons who read and commented upon several drafts of the *Handbook* and who offered us valuable advice and practical suggestions at various stages of its preparation: Frank N. Carney, Eric J. Carpenter, Gaetano Cipolla, Thomas Clayton, Robert A. Colby, Elizabeth W. Cowan, Gregory Cowan, Richard H. Cracroft, Marianna Davis, Robert J. Di Pietro, John H. Fisher, Jesse Gatlin, Mary W. George, John C. Gerber, Stirling Haig, Robert R. Hoyt, Richard A. LaFleur, Richard L. Larson, William T. Lenehan, William A. Little, Jane Marie Luecke, William D. Lutz, Michael H. Means, Harrison T. Meserole, George J. Metcalf, Neil E. Nakadate, Mary Ann O'Donnell, William H. Pell, James L. Rolleston, Jeffrey L. Sammons, Mina P. Shaughnessy, J. Kenneth Sieben, Adeline Skillman, Gayatri Chakravorty Spivak, David M. Staines, Rebecca M. Valette, Donald D. Walsh, Donna R. Walsh, Gerhard H. Weiss, Thomas M. Wilcox, Katharina Wilson, Linda L. Wyman, and Ella Mae York.

We would also like to give special thanks to Richard I. Brod, Claire Cook, Judy Goulding, Hilda Hanze, Carla Hayes, Kristin Helmers, Jeffrey Howitt, Cheryl Hurley, Linda J. Lehrer, Jasper P. Neel, Margot Rabiner, Hans Rütimann, Marjorie L. Rütimann, William D. Schaefer, and all our other colleagues on the MLA staff for their unfailing support and help.

Joseph Gibaldi
Walter S. Achtert

PREFACE FOR THE INSTRUCTOR AND THESIS ADVISER

The MLA Style Sheet (1951; rev. 1970) was compiled for literary and linguistic scholars who publish in learned journals. Its recommendations regarding the preparation of scholarly manuscripts have been so well received, however, that they have been adopted not only by journals and university presses but also by college departments and graduate schools. Hundreds of teachers have used the *Style Sheet* as the basis for their instructions about the form of research papers and theses, but, not surprisingly, many have complained about its inadequacy as a classroom text or as a supplementary reference guide. Thus the need has arisen for a handbook that would both incorporate the recommendations of the second edition of the *Style Sheet* and serve as a supplementary text in a writing course or as a reference book for undergraduate or graduate students to use independently.

The *MLA Handbook for Writers* attempts to meet that need. Every effort has been made to clarify the ambiguities of the revised *Style Sheet* and to amplify and illustrate matters only touched upon in the earlier work, where the reader's familiarity with the practices of scholarship was assumed. In addition, note and bibliographical specifications for types of sources not included in the second edition have been introduced. Many of these sources (e.g., films, radio and television programs, recordings) are becoming common references in research papers. The expanded section on bibliography includes a bibliographical listing for each kind of note reference given. To assist the student in spacing and indenting, examples have been reproduced in typescript, rather than set in type. The instructor who wishes to use the *MLA Handbook for Writers* as a text will find sections on selecting a topic, using the library, taking notes, outlining, and writing drafts, as well as instructions on the form of the paper—spacing, the insertion of quotations, the inclusion of tables and illustrations, pagination, and so on. An appendix dealing with the special problems of the dissertation is included for the graduate student.

As a handbook for writers of research papers, the *MLA Handbook* pays only minimal attention to the problems that writers of research papers share with all other writers. Questions of usage and writing style have been left, for the most part, to the many excellent manuals in that field.

PREFACE FOR THE STUDENT

The *MLA Handbook for Writers* describes a set of conventions governing the written presentation of research. Questions of writing style—choice of words, sentence structure, tone, and so on—are covered in other guides, such as those listed in Section 9, and are not considered here. The recommendations in this *Handbook* on the mechanics and format of the research paper are based upon the practices required by college teachers throughout the United States and Canada.

Sections 1 through 9 treat the logical steps in research and writing —selecting a topic, using the library, preparing a working bibliography, taking notes, avoiding plagiarism, outlining, and writing. Sections 10 through 17 are concerned with the mechanics of writing and cover such topics as quotations and titles in the text, punctuation, spelling, and capitalization. Sections 18 through 26 deal with the formal preparation of the manuscript—typing and binding the paper. Endnotes and footnotes are discussed in Sections 27 through 39, which provide well over a hundred examples illustrating citation forms for both printed sources and other sources often referred to in research papers (e.g., films and recordings). Sections 40 through 44, on the bibliography of the research paper, include sample bibliographical listings to parallel every type of note cited earlier. Sections 45 through 50, on abbreviations and reference words, are followed by an appendix on the preparation of theses and dissertations. An index and sample pages of a research paper conclude the book.

Like most reference works, the *MLA Handbook for Writers* contains information that ranges from the elementary to the esoteric. Thus it will be used differently by each reader. The undergraduate will probably wish to read carefully such basic sections as those on selecting a topic, using the library, and taking notes; the graduate student may wish to skip these and instead go directly to the more specialized sections, such as those on transliteration or the documentation of a book without page numbers but with signatures. For easy reference, the *Handbook* is divided into numbered sections and lettered subsections. The index refers to these sections and subsections, not to page numbers.

RESEARCH AND WRITING

1 THE RESEARCH PAPER

Like other forms of writing, the research paper should be characterized by lucid, coherent exposition. No set of conventions for preparing a manuscript can replace lively and intelligent writing. Unlike some other forms of writing, however, the research paper requires writers to seek out and investigate sources of information other than their own personal knowledge and experience. Research into a topic will yield new information, sharpen perception of a problem, and lend authority to some hypotheses. The research paper, the final product of research, is not a collection of other persons' opinions but a carefully constructed presentation of an idea—or series of ideas—that relies on other sources for clarification and verification. Learned facts and borrowed opinions must be fully documented in the research paper, usually through endnotes or footnotes, but always in such a manner that they support rather than overshadow the paper itself.

2 SELECTING A TOPIC

All writing begins with a topic. If you have some freedom in choosing a topic, look for one that interests you and that can be treated effectively within the imposed limits of time and space. "Twentieth-Century Literature" would not be a suitable choice for a term paper or even a dissertation. Students and scholars alike frequently begin with a fairly general topic and subsequently refine it, by research, into a more specific one. The student whose initial topic is "The Imagery of Wordsworth's *Prelude*," for instance, might, after some careful thought and reading, decide to focus on "Nature Imagery in Book I of Wordsworth's *Prelude*"; the topic "Modern Aviation" could be narrowed to "The SST and the Environment." (On selecting a dissertation topic, see Appendix, Sec. A.)

Before beginning any writing project, make sure you understand the amount and depth of research required, the degree of subjectivity permitted, and the type of paper expected—a report on the *process* (what you did) or the *product* (what you discovered) of your research.

3 USING THE LIBRARY

Many academic libraries offer programs of orientation and instruction to meet the needs of all students, the freshman as well as the doctoral candidate. Nearly all public and academic libraries have desks staffed by professional reference librarians who can help in locating information. These librarians can also provide information on the instructional programs offered by the library. An introduction to the library is provided in such books as Jean Key Gates, *Guide to the Use of Books and Libraries* (3rd ed., New York: McGraw-Hill, 1974) and Margaret Cook, *New Library Key* (3rd ed., New York: H. W. Wilson, 1975).

As a first step, students should learn to use the central card catalog of the library and become familiar with the two systems of classification most frequently used in American libraries: the Library of Congress and Dewey Decimal systems. They should also become acquainted with the range of reference works available, not only encyclopedias and dictionaries but periodical indexes, bibliographies, and abstracts that are kept in special sections or rooms. The *Readers' Guide to Periodical Literature* is an index to the contents of popular journals and magazines; the *New York Times Index* provides a guide to news stories and feature articles in that newspaper. Each subject area has its own specialized indexes: *L'Année Philologique* (for classical studies), *Applied Science and Technology Index, Art Index, Business Periodicals Index, Education Index, Humanities Index, Index to Religious Periodical Literature, MLA International Bibliography* (for modern languages and literatures), *Music Index,* and *Social Sciences Index*. Abstracting services provide useful summaries of the contents of journal articles: *Abstracts of English Studies, Biological Abstracts, Chemical Abstracts, Psychological Abstracts,* and *Sociological Abstracts* are a few of the reference works of this type.

Students should also learn where to find current periodicals, special collections (e.g., rare books or government documents), and copying facilities and how to use both a microfilm and a microfiche reader (perhaps even a microcard reader). Graduate students in particular should become familiar with interlibrary-loan procedures and any privileges available to those engaged in advanced study (e.g., carrel privileges).

4 COMPILING A WORKING BIBLIOGRAPHY

The first stage in research is to discover where to find useful information and opinions on your topic. Usually this involves compiling a "working bibliography"—a list of books, journal articles, recordings, and other sources that should be consulted. The working bibliography usually changes frequently during the research, reflecting a changing perception of the topic that develops through research, the discovery of possible new sources, and the discarding of sources that do not prove useful. The initial working bibliography is usually compiled from bibliographies and reference works like those mentioned in Sec. 3; additions are often made by noting the sources that these works have drawn upon (an article on Goethe located through the *MLA International Bibliography* may list in its notes books and other articles relevant to the topic).

In compiling a bibliography, make a note in a shortened form of the exact source of each reference (MLA Bib., 74, I, 2333 would suffice for *1974 MLA International Bibliography,* Volume I, item 2333). This record is essential when items must be borrowed from other institutions, since a printed source of information is always required for verification before an interlibrary loan may be requested. Keeping track of which tools have been consulted also helps the researcher become aware of the most fruitful resources.

5 TAKING NOTES

Although everyone agrees that note-taking is essential to scholarly study, probably no two students or scholars employ identical methods of taking notes. Some use index cards; others use notebooks, beginning each new entry on a fresh page; still others use loose-leaf pages clipped together according to one system or another. Regardless of the method, take down all the information you will need for documentation and bibliography (see Secs. 31, 33, 35, and 41). Although you may paraphrase or summarize ideas when the original wording is not of prime importance, transcribe exactly, word for word, all material that you might want to quote directly, in whole or in part, in the research paper. Be sure to use quotation marks scrupulously in your notes to distinguish between verbatim quotation and paraphrase. Cite page numbers accurately for both. When a quotation continues to another page, be careful to note where the page break occurs, since only a small portion of what is transcribed may ultimately find its way into the paper.

6 PLAGIARISM

Derived from the Latin word *plagiarius* ("kidnapper" and also "plagiarist" in the modern sense), plagiarism is defined by Alexander Lindley as "the false assumption of authorship: the wrongful act of taking the product of another person's mind, and presenting it as one's own" (*Plagiarism and Originality* [New York: Harper, 1952], p. 2). Plagiarism may take the form of repeating another's sentences as your own, adopting a particularly apt phrase as your own, paraphrasing someone else's argument as your own, or even presenting someone else's line of thinking in the development of a thesis as though it were your own. In short, to plagiarize is to give the impression that you have written or thought something that you have in fact borrowed from another. Although a writer may use other persons' words and thoughts, they must be acknowledged as such. The following passage appears in Volume I of the *Literary History of the United States*:

The major concerns of Dickinson's poetry early and late, her "flood subjects," may be defined as the seasons and nature, death and a problematic afterlife, the kinds and phases of love, and poetry as the divine art.

The following, given without documentation, constitutes plagiarism:

The chief subjects of Emily Dickinson's poetry

include nature and the seasons, death and the afterlife, the various types and stages of love, and poetry itself as a divine art.

But one may write the following with an accompanying note:

Text:
It has been suggested that the chief subjects of Emily Dickinson's poetry include nature, death, love, and poetry as a divine art.[1]

Note (see Sec. 30 on the placement of notes):

[1] William M. Gibson and Stanley T. Williams, "Experiments in Poetry: Emily Dickinson and Sidney Lanier," in <u>Literary History of the United States</u>, ed. Robert E. Spiller et al., 4th ed. (New York: Macmillan, 1974), I, 906.

If there is doubt concerning plagiarism, cite the source or sources. On common knowledge and note logic, see Sec. 28.

7 OUTLINING

Many writers find that an outline or a brief prospectus is a necessary intermediate step between the research and writing stages. The outline helps the writer organize ideas and accumulated research into a logical, coherent whole. Some instructors require that an outline be submitted with a research paper. With theses and dissertations, it is common for advisers and readers to insist on seeing a detailed outline before permitting a student to begin writing. Descending parts of an outline are normally labeled in the following order: I, A, 1, a, (1), (a). Logic requires, of course, that there be a "II" to complement a "I," a "B" to complement an "A," and so forth, and also that the coordinate parts of an outline be in parallel form (if "A" is followed by a sentence, then so should "B"; if "A" is followed by a phrase, then so should "B").

8 WRITING DRAFTS

Writers are rarely satisfied with the expression of their ideas as first set down. Most begin with a quickly executed first draft that follows their outline and presents their ideas in rough form. In subsequent drafts, they may add or delete material, improve the wording, make the style consistent, and correct mechanical errors. The number of drafts depends upon the time allowed for a project and the personal standards of the writer.

9 GUIDES TO WRITING

Effective writing depends as much on clarity and readability as on content. Grammar and diction, usage and sentence structure are important considerations, as are the mechanics of writing—punctuation, capitalization, spelling, and so on. In recent years, writers, teachers, and publishers have also become increasingly concerned about the social implications of language. The careful writer not only avoids unsubstantiated generalizations about persons on the basis of factors such as age, economic class, national origin, political and religious beliefs, race, and sex but also gives consideration to the implications of language. For example, many writers now avoid the use of the generic pronoun "he" in referring to a person whose sex is not specified so as to avoid the possible implication that only a male person is intended. For advice on current practices, consult an instructor or one of the more recent guides listed below.

A good dictionary is an essential tool for any writer. An instructor can recommend a standard American dictionary such as the *American College Dictionary, American Heritage Dictionary of the English Language, Random House Dictionary of the English Language,* or *Webster's New Collegiate Dictionary* (the Oxford dictionaries record British spelling).

Because standard dictionaries vary in matters such as hyphenation and preferred spelling of words, use one dictionary throughout to maintain consistency. Students who will frequently be using a language other than English should invest in a standard dictionary of that language. In all cases, avoid inexpensive dictionaries, which are often too incomplete to be of more than rudimentary help.

Instructors should also be consulted on the choice of a reliable guide to writing, of which many are available. For the benefit of readers not currently enrolled in a writing course, a selected list of such guides appears below. The first group consists of standard handbooks of composition; the second, of dictionaries of modern usage; and the third, of books dealing primarily with matters such as tone, voice, and style.

I

Baker, Sheridan. *The Practical Stylist*. 3rd ed. New York: T. Y. Crowell, 1973.

Crews, Frederick. *The Random House Handbook*. 2nd ed. New York: Random House, 1977.

Elsbree, Langdon, and Frederick Bracher. *Heath's College Handbook of Composition*. 8th ed. Lexington, Mass.: D. C. Heath, 1972.

Gorrell, Robert M., and Charlton Laird. *Modern English Handbook*, 6th ed. Englewood Cliffs, N.J.: Prentice-Hall, 1976.

Guth, Hans P. *Words and Ideas: A Handbook for College Writing*. 4th ed. Belmont, Calif.: Wadsworth, 1972.

Hodges, John C., and Mary E. Whitten. *Harbrace College Handbook*. 7th ed. New York: Harcourt Brace Jovanovich, 1972.

Irmscher, W. F. *The Holt Guide to English: A Contemporary Handbook of Rhetoric, Language, and Literature*. 2nd ed. New York: Holt, Rinehart and Winston, 1976.

Kierzek, John M., and Walker Gibson. *Macmillan Handbook of English*. 5th ed. New York: Macmillan, 1965.

Leggett, Glenn, C. David Mead, and William Charvat. *Prentice-Hall Handbook for Writers*. 6th ed. Englewood Cliffs, N.J.: Prentice-Hall, 1974.

Marckwardt, Albert H., and Frederic G. Cassidy. *Scribner Handbook of English*. 4th ed. New York: Scribners, 1967.

McCrimmon, James M. *Writing with a Purpose*. 6th ed. Boston: Houghton Mifflin, 1975.

Perrin, Porter G., and Wilma R. Ebbitt. *Writer's Guide and Index to English*. 5th ed. Chicago: Scott, Foresman, 1972.

Watkins, Floyd C., William B. Dillingham, and Edwin T. Martin. *Practical English Handbook*. 4th ed. Boston: Houghton Mifflin, 1974.

II

Bernstein, Theodore M. *The Careful Writer: A Modern Guide to English Usage*. New York: Atheneum, 1965.

Bryant, Margaret M., ed. *Current American Usage: How Americans Say It and Write It*. New York: Funk and Wagnalls, 1962.

Copperud, Roy H. *American Usage: The Consensus*. New York: Van Nostrand Reinhold, 1970.

Follett, Wilson. *Modern American Usage: A Guide*. Ed. Jacques Barzun. New York: Hill and Wang, 1966.

Fowler, Henry W. *A Dictionary of Modern English Usage*. Ed. Ernest Gowers. 2nd ed. New York: Oxford Univ. Press, 1965.

Nicholson, Margaret. *A Dictionary of American-English Usage Based on Fowler's* Modern English Usage. New York: Oxford Univ. Press, 1957.

III

Beardsley, Monroe C. *Thinking Straight: Principles of Reasoning for Readers and Writers*. 4th ed. Englewood Cliffs, N.J.: Prentice-Hall, 1975.

Cowan, Gregory, and Elizabeth McPherson. *Plain English Please*. 3rd ed. New York: Random House, 1976.

Eastman, Richard M. *Style: Writing as the Discovery of Outlook*. New York: Oxford Univ. Press, 1970.

Elbow, Peter. *Writing without Teachers*. New York: Oxford Univ. Press, 1975.

Gibson, Walker. *Tough, Sweet and Stuffy: An Essay on Modern American Prose Styles*. Bloomington: Indiana Univ. Press, 1966.

Gowers, Ernest. *The Complete Plain Words*. Ed. Bruce Fraser. 2nd ed. Baltimore: Penguin, 1975.

Lanham, Richard A. *Style: An Anti-Textbook*. New Haven: Yale Univ. Press, 1974.

MacRorie, Ken. *Telling Writing*. 2nd ed. Rochelle Park, N.J.: Hayden, 1976.

Smith, Charles K. *Styles and Structures: Alternative Approaches to Student Writing*. New York: Norton, 1974.

Stewart, Donald C. *The Authentic Voice: A Pre-Writing Approach to Student Writing*. Dubuque, Iowa: Wm. C. Brown, 1972.

Strunk, William, Jr., and E. B. White. *The Elements of Style*. 2nd ed. New York: Macmillan, 1972.

White, Edward M. *The Writer's Control of Tone*. New York: Norton, 1970.

MECHANICS OF WRITING

10 PUNCTUATION

a. General remarks. The primary purpose of punctuation is to ensure the clarity and readability of your writing. Although there are many required uses, punctuation is, to some extent, a matter of personal preference. But, while certain practices are optional, consistency is mandatory. Writers must guard against adopting different styles in parallel situations. The remarks below stress the conventions that pertain especially to research papers. More comprehensive discussions of punctuation can be found in standard handbooks of composition, such as those listed in Sec. 9.

b. Apostrophes indicate contractions (rarely acceptable in scholarly writing) and possessives. General practice is to form the possessive of monosyllabic proper names ending in a sibilant sound (s, z, sh, zh, ch, j) by adding an apostrophe and another *s* (Keats's poems, Marx's theories) except, by convention, for names in classical literature (Mars' wrath). In words of more than one syllable ending in a sibilant, only the apostrophe is added (Hopkins' poems, Cervantes' *novelas*) except for names ending in a sibilant and a final *e* (Horace's odes). Note that the possessive of a name ending with a silent *s* is formed by adding an apostrophe and another *s* (Camus's novels).

c. Colons are used to indicate that what follows will be an example, explanation, or elaboration of what has just been said. They are commonly used to introduce quotations (see Secs. 14b, 14c, and 14f). For their use in documentation and bibliography, see Secs. 31c, 31h, and 41c. Always skip one space after a colon.

d. Commas are usually required between items in a series (blood, sweat, and tears), between coordinate adjectives (an absorbing, frightening account), before coordinating conjunctions joining independent clauses, around parenthetical elements, and after fairly long phrases or clauses preceding the main clause of a sentence. They are also conventional in dates (January 1, 1980), names (W. K. Wimsatt, Jr., and Walter J. Ong, S.J.), and addresses (Brooklyn, New York). A comma and a dash are never used together in modern English usage. If the context requires a comma (as it does here), the comma follows a closing parenthesis, but a comma never precedes an opening parenthesis. See Secs. 31, 33, 35, and 41 for the uses of the comma in documentation and bibliography; see Sec. 14f for commas with quotation marks.

e. Dashes. A dash is typed as two hyphens, with no space before or after. Some writers tend to overuse dashes, substituting them loosely for other marks of punctuation. The dash, however, has only a few legitimate uses: around parenthetical elements that represent a break in the flow of thought, around parenthetical elements that require a number of internal commas, and before a summarizing appositive.

```
Carter's sweep of the South--Virginia was the only
Southern state to vote Republican--helped give him
the election.
```

```
Many twentieth-century American writers--Faulkner,
Capote, Styron, Williams, to name only a few--come
from the South.
```

```
Stray dogs, abandoned cats, injured birds,
orphaned baby rabbits--all found a home with us.
```

See Sec. 39 for use of the dash in documentation.

f. Exclamation marks should be used sparingly in **scholarly** writing.

g. Hyphens are used to form some types of compound words, particularly compound adjectives that precede the word(s) they modify (a mind-boggling experience, a well-established policy, a first-rate study). Hyphens also join prefixes to capitalized words (post-Renaissance) and link pairs of coequal nouns (poet-priest, teacher-scholar). Many other compounds, however, are written as one word (wordplay, storytelling) or as two (social security tax, a happily married man). Consult a standard dictionary or writing manual for guidance in determining which compounds require hyphenation. Hyphens are also used to connect numbers indicating a range (pp. 1-20). For the use of hyphens in dates, see Sec. 11c; for hyphens in unavoidable word divisions at the end of a line, see Sec. 12b.

h. Italics (underlining). Avoid frequent use of italics (underlining in typing) for emphasis. (On the underlining of titles, see Sec. 13.) Phrases, words, or letters cited as linguistic examples and foreign words used in English text are underlined. The numerous exceptions to this last rule include quotations entirely in another language, titles of articles in another language (placed within quotation marks), proper names, and foreign words anglicized through frequent usage. Since American English rapidly naturalizes words, use a dictionary and your own knowledge of current usage to determine which originally foreign expressions still require italics. Much, of course, depends on the audience. Foreign words, abbreviations, and phrases commonly not underlined include: etc., e.g., et al., laissez faire, raison d'être, tête-à-tête, and versus. In discussions of the arts, such words or expressions as the following are also not underlined: cliché, enjambment, genre, hubris, leitmotif, mimesis, and roman à clef. (On italicizing abbreviations, see Sec. 47.)

i. Parentheses are used to enclose parenthetical remarks and to enclose some items in documentation (see Secs. 31h, 33f, 37, and 41c). On parenthetical documentation, see Sec. 39.

j. Periods end sentences. They also come at the end of notes and after complete blocks of information in bibliographical citations (see Sec. 41). The period follows a parenthesis that falls at the end of a sentence. It is placed within the parenthesis when the parenthetical element is independent (see, not this sentence, but the next). (For the use of periods with ellipsis, see Sec. 14d; for periods within quotation marks, see Sec. 14f.)

k. Quotation marks. Enclose in double quotation marks words to which attention is being directed (e.g., words purposely misused or used in a special sense, words referred to as words, and parenthetical English translations of words or phrases from another language). Note, however, that words used as examples in linguistic studies are underlined and not enclosed in double quotation marks (see Sec. 10h). Use single quotation marks for definitions or translations that appear without intervening punctuation (e.g., *ainsi* 'thus'). For the use of quotation marks with titles, see Sec. 13; and, for use of single and double quotation marks in quoted material, see Sec. 14f.

l. Semicolons are used to separate items in a series when some of the items require internal commas. They are used between independent clauses that are not joined by a coordinating conjunction, and they may be used before the coordinating conjunction in a compound sentence if one of the independent clauses requires a number of internal commas. For the use of semicolons in documentation and bibliography, see Secs. 31e, 32k, 36, 37, and 42k.

m. Slashes (virgules) are used to separate lines of poetry (see Sec. 14b) and elements of dates (see Sec. 11c), to enclose phonemic transcription, and occasionally to separate alternative words (and/or).

n. Square brackets, to be inserted by hand if they are not on the typewriter, are used for an unavoidable parenthesis within a parenthesis, to enclose interpolations in a quotation (see Sec. 14e) or in incomplete data (see sample notes 58 and 64 in Secs. 32r and 32t), and to enclose phonetic transcription.

11 NUMERALS

a. In general, numbers that cannot be spelled out in one or two words may be written as numerals (one, thirty-six, ninety-nine, one hundred, two thousand, three million; but 2½, 101, 137, and 1,275). Numbers compared or contrasted should be in the same style (5 out of 125, 2½ to 3 years old or two-and-a-half to three years old). In technical or statistical discussions involving their frequent use or in notes, where many space-saving devices are legitimate, all numbers may be written as numerals. Common practice is to put a comma between the third and fourth digits from the right, the sixth and seventh, and so on.

```
1,000    20,000    7,654,321
```

Exceptions to this practice include page and line numbers of four or more digits, addresses, and year numbers. The comma is added in year numbers if a fifth digit is used.

```
On page 3333. . . .

At 4132 Broadway. . . .

In 1984. . . .
```
but
```
In 20,000 B.C. . . .
```

Never use a capital "I" for the Arabic numeral one. If the typewriter does not have the number "1," use a small letter el ("l"). Dates and page numbers are rarely spelled out: "12 April" or "April 12" and "page 45" are generally preferred to "the twelfth of April" and "the forty-fifth page." Because numbers beginning sentences (including dates) are, by convention, spelled out, avoid beginning a sentence with a number.

b. Percentages and amounts of money are treated as other numbers: if the numbers involved cannot be spelled out in one or two words, they may be written as numerals with the appropriate symbols (one percent, forty-five percent, one hundred percent, five dollars, thirty-five dollars, two thousand dollars, sixty-eight cents; but 2½%, 150%, $2.65, $303, £127). In business, scientific, and technical writing involving their frequent use, all percentages and amounts of money may be written as numerals with the appropriate symbols.

c. Dates. As in other aspects of writing, be consistent in expressing dates: either "22 July 1981" or "July 22, 1981," but not both (if the latter, be sure to put a comma both before and after the year unless another punctuation mark is required); either "August 1981" or "August, 1981," but not both. Centuries are written out in lowercase letters (the twentieth century). A hyphen is added if the century is being used as an adjective (eighteenth-century thought; nineteenth- and twentieth-century literature). Decades are also usually written out without capitalization (the seventies), but it is becoming acceptable to express them in figures (the 1970s). "B.C." follows the year, but "A.D." precedes it (19 B.C.; A.D. 565). (Some writers use "B.C.E.," before the Common Era, and "C.E.," Common Era.) European usage gives all dates in day-month-year order, separated by spaces, commas, hyphens, periods, or slash marks (2 March 1974, 2-3-74, 2/III/74). To indicate both Western and non-Western dates, put one set in parentheses: "3 November 1693 (K'ang hsi 32/10/6)." Both "in 1951-52" and "from 1951 to 1952" are clear and acceptable, as is "from 1951-52 to 1968-69," but "from 1951-72" alone is not because, lacking the preposition "to" after "1951," the phrase is inaccurate and confusing.

d. Inclusive numbers. In connecting consecutive numbers, give the second number in full for numbers through ninety-nine. For larger numbers, give only the last two figures of the second if it is within the same hundred or thousand: pp. 2-3, 10-12, 21-28, 103-04, 395-401, 923-1003, 1003-05, 1608-774, 1999-2004, 12345-47, 12345-3300.

e. Roman numerals. Use capital Roman numerals for primary divisions of an outline (see Sec. 7), books and parts of a work, volumes, acts of a play, or individuals in a series.

Book I of Spenser's <u>Faerie Queene</u>

Part II of Goethe's <u>Faust</u>

Volume II of <u>Encyclopedia Americana</u>

Act III of <u>Arms and the Man</u>

Elizabeth II

Use lowercase Roman numerals for chapters of a book (Chapter xii), scenes of a play (Act I, Scene ii), cantos of a poem (Book I, Canto iv), chapters of books of the Bible (Luke xiv), and the preliminary pages of a dissertation (e.g., preface, table of contents). On capitalization, see Sec. 15. On the use of Roman numerals in documentation, see Secs. 31i and 31j.

12 SPELLING

a. General remarks. Spelling, including hyphenation, must be consistent, except in quotations: quoted material must be reproduced exactly as it appears in the original. See Sec. 9 on the selection and use of a dictionary.

b. Word division. Avoid dividing words at the end of a line. Where divisions are unavoidable, practice in the United States is to divide words according to pronunciation ("rep-re-sent"), whereas the British divide according to word derivation ("re-pre-sent"). Other languages have their own rules for dividing words: French, for instance, usually divides on a vowel ("ho-mé-rique"; in English, "Ho-mer-ic"). If in doubt, consult a dictionary.

c. Accents. In quoting, reproduce all accents exactly as they appear in the original. Bear in mind that in French, when capital letters are followed by lowercase letters, the capital letters are not always accented (always "école," but "Ecole" is acceptable). Although it is never unacceptable to place an accent over a capital letter that would require one if it were lowercase, the practice of French printers varies when words appear entirely in capital letters: *À, É, È, Ù,* and capital letters bearing a circumflex are often accented, but often not. When transcribing words that appear in all capitals and changing them to lowercase, insert the necessary accents.

Accent marks should be written in by hand if the typewriter does not have them. Students using languages in which frequent use of accents is required should consider purchasing a typewriter with an international keyboard or having their typewriters modified.

d. Dieresis. In German words the dieresis, not *e*, should be used for the umlaut (ä, ö, ü *rather than* ae, oe, ue), even for initial capitals ("Über"). But common usage must be observed for names: Götz, but Goethe.

e. Digraphs. A digraph is a combination of two letters that represents only one sound (e.g., *th, oa* in "broad"). In many languages, some digraphs appear united in print (æ, œ, β). They may be transcribed in typescript without any connection between them (ae, oe, ss). (Some prefer to reproduce the united digraph as closely as possible by writing in the character or by joining the tops of the two typed letters.) In American English, the digraph *ae* is slowly being abandoned in favor of the *e* alone; "encyclopedia" and "archeology" (instead of "encyclopaedia" and "archaeology") and "esthetic" and "medieval" are now acceptable.

13 TITLES IN THE TEXT

For capitalization of titles, see Sec. 15.

a. Underlined. Titles of published books, plays (of any length), long poems (usually poems that have been published as books), pamphlets, periodicals (including newspapers and magazines), works of classical literature (but not sacred writings), films, radio and television programs, ballets, operas, instrumental music (but not if identified simply by form, number, and key), paintings, sculpture, and names of ships and aircraft are all underlined in the text. Although some contend that underlining only words is more pleasing esthetically than underlining both words and intervening spaces, either practice is permissible.

David Copperfield (published book)

As You Like It (play)

The Waste Land (long poem)

New Jersey Driver Manual (pamphlet)

Washington Post (newspaper)

Time (magazine)

Horace's Ars Poetica (work of classical literature)

Sounder (film)

All in the Family (television program)

Giselle (ballet)

Rigoletto (opera)

Berlioz' Symphonie fantastique (instrumental music
  identified by name)

Beethoven's Symphony No. 7 in A (instrumental music
  identified by form, number, and key)

Chagall's I and My Village (painting)

Bernini's Ecstasy of St. Theresa (sculpture)

H.M.S. Vanguard (ship)

Spirit of St. Louis (aircraft)

b. In quotation marks. Titles of articles, essays, short stories, short poems, songs, chapters of books, unpublished works (such as dissertations), lectures and speeches, courses, and individual episodes of radio and television programs are enclosed in quotation marks.

"Sharp Rise in Unemployment"   (article in a newspaper)

"Sources of Energy in the Twenty-First Century"

    (article in a magazine)

"The Writer's Audience Is Always a Fiction"   (article

    in a scholarly journal)

"Etruscan"   (encyclopedia article)

"The Fiction of Langston Hughes"   (essay in a book)

"Young Goodman Brown"   (short story)

"Kubla Khan"   (poem)

"Summertime"   (song)

"Italian Literature before Dante"   (chapter in a book)

"Goethe's _Faust_ and the German Puppet-Play"

    (unpublished dissertation)

"The Style and the Story: Shakespeare's Appropriate

    and Varying Artistry"   (lecture)

"Introductory Mathematics"   (course)

"The Joy Ride"   (episode of the television program _Upstairs,_

    Downstairs)

c. Titles within titles. If a title indicated by quotation marks appears within an underlined title, the quotation marks are retained. If a title indicated by underlining appears within a title enclosed in quotation marks, the underlining is retained.

<u>"Young Goodman Brown" and Hawthorne's Puritan</u>

    <u>Heritage</u>   (book)

"<u>As You Like It</u> as a Pastoral Poem"   (article)

When a title normally indicated by quotation marks appears within another title requiring quotation marks, the shorter title is given single quotation marks.

"An Interpretation of Coleridge's 'Kubla Khan'"

  (article)

When a normally underlined title appears within another underlined title, the shorter title appears neither underlined nor in quotation marks.

<u>The Art of</u> David Copperfield   (book)

d. Exceptions. These conventions of underlining titles or placing them within quotation marks do not apply to sacred writings (including all books and versions of the Bible), to series, editions, and societies, to descriptive words or phrases (or conventional titles) used instead of an actual title, and to parts of a book, none of which is underlined or put within quotation marks. (On capitalization, see Sec. 15.)

Sacred writings:

Bible

King James Version

Old Testament

Genesis

Gospels

Talmud

Koran

Upanishads

Series:

Bollingen Series

University of North Carolina Studies in

  Comparative Literature

```
Masterpiece Theatre
```

Editions:
```
New Variorum Edition of Shakespeare
```
```
Centenary Edition of the Works of Nathaniel
```
```
   Hawthorne
```

Societies:
```
American Medical Association
```
```
Renaissance Society of America
```

Descriptive words or phrases or conventional titles:
```
Roosevelt's first Inaugural Address
```
```
Mona Lisa   [for Leonardo da Vinci's La Gioconda]
```

Parts of a book:
```
Introduction
```
```
Preface
```
```
Appendix
```
```
Index
```

e. Frequent use of a title. If a title is to be mentioned often in the text, after the first full reference in the text or in a note, use only a shortened (if possible, familiar or obvious) title or abbreviation (e.g., "Nightingale" for "Ode to a Nightingale"; *Much Ado* for *Much Ado about Nothing*; HEW for Department of Health, Education, and Welfare). This practice is also followed in notes (see Sec. 37).

14 QUOTATIONS

a. In general, all quotations—whether a word, phrase, sentence, paragraph, or more—should correspond exactly to the original source in spelling, capitalization, and interior punctuation (on the use of ellipsis, see Sec. 14d). Exceptions, such as the underlining of words for emphasis or the modernization of spelling, must be explicitly indicated or explained in a note or enclosed in parentheses at the end of the quotation or in square brackets within the quotation (on the uses of parentheses and square brackets, see Secs. 10i and 10n):

Lincoln specifically advocated a government "for

the people" (emphasis added).

Take care to ensure that the syntax of your sentence accords grammatically with that of the quotation.

b. Poetry. Unless unusual emphasis is required, verse quotations of a single line or part of a line should be incorporated, within quotation marks, as part of the text. Quotations of two or three lines may also be placed in the text, within quotation marks, but with the lines separated by a slash (/), with a space on each side of the slash.

In Shakespeare's Julius Caesar, Antony says of

Brutus, "This was the noblest Roman of them all."

In Julius Caesar, Antony begins his famous

speech: "Friends, Romans, countrymen, lend me your

ears; / I come to bury Caesar, not to praise

him."

Verse quotations of more than three lines should be separated from the text by triple-spacing, introduced in most cases by a colon, indented ten spaces from the left margin (or less if the lines quoted are unusually long, so that a ten-space indentation would make the page look unbalanced), and typed with double-spacing (single-spacing for dissertations) but without quotation marks unless they appear in the original. The spatial arrangement of the original (including indentation and spacing within and between lines) should be reproduced as accurately as possible.

Crashaw begins his poem "The Weeper" with several
metaphors describing the eyes of St. Mary
Magdalene, withholding until the end of the first
stanza the subject of his work:

> Haile, Sister Springs,
> Parents of Silver-footed rills!
> Ever bubling things!
> Thawing Crystall! Snowy hills!
> Still spending, never spent; I meane
> Thy faire eyes, sweet <u>Magdalen</u>.

If the quotation begins in the middle of the line of verse, it
should be reproduced as such and not shifted to the left margin.

It is in Act II of <u>As You Like It</u> that Jaques is
given the speech that many think contains a
glimpse of Shakespeare's conception of drama:

> All the world's a stage
> And all the men and women merely players:
> They have their exits and their
>   entrances;
> And one man in his time plays many parts,
> His acts being seven ages.

Jaques then proceeds to enumerate and analyze
these ages.

c. Prose. Prose quotations of not more than four lines in the typescript, unless special emphasis is required, should always be incorporated, within quotation marks, as part of the text.

For Dickens it was both "the best of times" and

"the worst of times."

"He was obeyed," writes Conrad of the Company

manager in <u>Heart of Darkness</u>, "yet he inspired

neither love nor fear, nor even respect."

Longer quotations (more than four lines in the typescript) are usually introduced by a colon or comma (see Sec. 14f), set off from the text by triple-spacing, indented ten spaces from the left margin, and typed with double-spacing (single-spacing for dissertations) but without quotation marks. If a single paragraph, or part of one, is quoted, do not indent the first line more than the body of the quotation; if two or more paragraphs are quoted consecutively (as in the following example), indent the first line of each an additional three spaces. If, however, the first sentence quoted is not the beginning of a paragraph in the source, do not indent it the additional three spaces.

In <u>Moll Flanders</u>, Defoe maintains the

pseudo-autobiographical narration typical of the

picaresque tradition:

      My true name is so well known in the

    records or registers at Newgate, and in

    the Old Bailey, and there are some things

    of such consequence still depending

    there, relating to my particular conduct,

    that it is not to be expected I should

```
set my name or the account of my family

to this work.  Perhaps, after my death,

it may be better known; at present it

would not be proper, no, not tho' a

general pardon should be issued, even

without exceptions of persons or crimes.

    It is enough to tell you, that . . .

some of my worst comrades, who are out

of the way of doing me harm, having gone

out of the world by the steps and the

string as I often expected to go, knew

me by the name of Moll Flanders. . . .
```

d. Ellipsis. When omitting a word, phrase, sentence, or paragraph from a quoted passage, writers should be guided by two principles: (1) fairness to the author being quoted and (2) clarity and correct grammar in their own writing. If only a fragment of a sentence is quoted, it will be obvious that some of the original sentence has been left out: In his Inaugural Address, Kennedy spoke of a "new frontier." But if, after material from the original has been omitted, the quotation appears to be a grammatical sentence or a series of grammatical sentences, the omission (or omissions) should be indicated by using ellipsis points (i.e., spaced periods). For ellipsis *within* a sentence, use three such periods (. . .), leaving a space before and after each period. A quotation that can stand as a complete sentence should end with a period even if something in the original has been omitted. When the ellipsis coincides with the end of your sentence, use three *spaced* periods *following* a sentence period (i.e., four periods, with no space before the first). If parenthetical material follows the ellipsis at the end of your sentence, use three *spaced* periods and place the sentence period after the final parenthesis.

Original:

The sense of isolation present in many of the poems of his earlier
collections grew into an obsessive loneliness, under the pressure of
two alien cultures. (From Robert Pring-Mill, *Pablo Neruda: A Basic
Anthology* [Oxford: Dolphin, 1975], p. xxi.)

Quoted with ellipsis in the middle:

As Robert Pring-Mill notes of Neruda's years in the

East, "The sense of isolation . . . grew into an

obsessive loneliness, under the pressure of two

alien cultures."

Quoted with ellipsis at the end:

As Robert Pring-Mill notes of Neruda's years in the

East, "The sense of isolation present in many of

the poems of his earlier collections grew into an

obsessive loneliness. . . ."

or

As Robert Pring-Mill notes of Neruda's years in the

East, "The sense of isolation present in many of

the poems of his earlier collections grew into an

obsessive loneliness . . ." (p. xxi).

Four periods may also be used to indicate the omission of a
whole sentence or more or of a paragraph or more. Remember,
however, that grammatically complete sentences must both
precede and follow the four periods. (Where the extent of the
omission is significant—when, for example, several pages separate two quoted paragraphs—the ellipsis may be indicated by
a single typed line of spaced periods.)

Original:

The most dissimilar people said similar if not identical things about
this unique soul, this poet who gave so much delight. They spoke of
his wonderfully balanced humanity, the expanse and gentleness of his

spirit and his incredibly subtle art. All testify that he taught his contemporaries to see things, to recognise relationships, to love what is fine, to be aware of depths, and to discover the hidden ways of the human soul, and that he did this with a gentle but sure conviction. (From J. R. von Salis, *Rainer Maria Rilke: The Years in Switzerland,* trans. N. K. Cruickshank [Berkeley: Univ. of California Press, 1966], p. 290.)

Quoted:

J. R. von Salis has written of Rilke, "The most

dissimilar people said similar if not identical

things about this unique soul. . . . All testify

that he taught his contemporaries to see things, to

recognise relationships, to love what is fine, to

be aware of depths. . . ."

Some scholars prefer to indicate whether what is omitted is the last part of one sentence or the first part of the next sentence by leaving a space before the first period if the last word of the first sentence is not quoted.

The accuracy of the quotation and the exact reproduction of the original are paramount in scholarly writing. Unless indicated in brackets, liberties must not be taken with the spelling or punctuation of the original. The writer must construct sentences that allow, on the one hand, for the exactness of the quotation and, on the other, for clarity and correct grammatical structure. In many cases, it is best simply to paraphrase, grammatically incorporating fragments of the original into the text.

Original:

Moralists have unanimously agreed, that unless virtue be nursed by liberty, it will never attain due strength—and what they say of man I extend to mankind, insisting that in all cases morals must be fixed on immutable principles; and, that the being cannot be termed rational or virtuous, who obeys any authority, but that of reason. (From Mary Wollstonecraft, *A Vindication of the Rights of Woman,* ed. Carol H. Poston [New York: Norton, 1975], Ch. xiii, Sec. 6 [p. 191].)

Quoted:

"[U]nless virtue be nursed by liberty," wrote Mary

Wollstonecraft, "it will never attain due

strength. . . ."

But writers who prefer not to use square brackets to indicate
the changing of a lowercase letter into uppercase should recast
the sentence:

Mary Wollstonecraft wrote that "unless virtue be

nursed by liberty, it will never attain due

strength. . . ."

e. Interpolations. The writer's own comments or explana-
tions *within* quotations are enclosed in square brackets (*not
parentheses*), which are often not included on typewriters and
may have to be inserted by hand. Use "sic" ("thus," "so")
sparingly—in square brackets and without quotation marks or
an exclamation point—to assure readers that the quotation is
accurate although the spelling or logic might lead them to
doubt it. Unless the writer states otherwise (e.g., by "emphasis added"; see Sec. 14a), the reader will assume that whatever is underlined in the quotation was italicized or underlined
in the original.

The term paper was entitled "On Wordsworth's

'Imitations of Immorality' [sic]."

Hamlet says of his mother:

        Why, she would hang on him

    [Hamlet's father]

    As if increase of appetite had grown

    By what it fed on. . . .

f. Punctuating quotations. Quotations set off from the text require no quotation marks; internal punctuation should be reproduced exactly as in the original. For quotations included as part of the text, first use double quotation marks, then, for quotations within quotations, single marks:

```
The professor in the novel confessed that he found
it "impossible to teach the 'To be or not to be'
speech" because he was himself terrified by its
implications.
```

Commas and periods are placed *inside* closing quotation marks unless a parenthetical or bracketed reference intervenes. (If a quotation ends with both a single and a double quotation mark, the comma or period is placed within both: "Read 'Kubla Khan,' " he told me.) All other punctuation goes outside quotation marks, except when it is part of the matter quoted.

Original:
I believe taxation without representation is tyranny!

Quoted:
```
He attacked "taxation without representation."

He attacked "taxation without representation" (p.
32).

Did he attack "taxation without representation"?

He did not even attack "taxation without
representation"!
```
but
```
He declared that "taxation without representation
is tyranny!"
```

When a quotation is formally introduced, it is preceded by a colon. Quotations of verse are also usually preceded by a colon.

Coleridge's <u>Rime of the Ancient Mariner</u> concludes:

"A sadder and a wiser man, / He rose the morrow

morn."
but
"Poets," according to Shelley, "are the

unacknowledged legislators of the world."

5 CAPITALIZATION

a. English. In all English titles, not only of entire works (such as novels, lectures, or essays) but also of divisions of works (such as parts or chapters), capitalize the first letter of the first word, the last word, and all the principal words—including nouns and adjectives in hyphenated compounds but excluding articles, prepositions (except when they function as adverbs), conjunctions, and the "to" in infinitives.

<u>Death of a Salesman</u>

<u>Antony and Cleopatra</u>

<u>The Hero in Nineteenth-Century Novels: A Survey</u>

<u>The Teaching of Spanish in English-Speaking

Countries</u>

"Ode to a Nightingale"

"Italian Literature before Dante"

"The Life Beyond"

"What Americans Stand For"

In references to magazines or newspapers (the *Washington*

Post), the initial definite article is usually not treated as part of the title. The words "series" and "edition" are capitalized only when they are considered part of an exact title (the Norton Critical Edition, the Twayne World Authors Series, *but* Penguin edition, the Studies in English Literature series). Titles like Preface, Introduction, and Appendix are often capitalized, particularly when they refer to a well-known work, such as Wordsworth's Preface to *Lyrical Ballads*. They are also capitalized when formally cited in notes and bibliographies (see Sec. 31b). In many other contexts, however, these terms need not be treated as titles (the author claims in an introduction). Capitalize and, in documentation, abbreviate a noun followed by a numeral indicating place in a sequence: Vol. II of 3 vols., Pl. 4, No. 20, Act V, Ch. iii, Version A. Do not capitalize col., fol., l., n., p., or sig. (see Sec. 48 for the meanings of these and other abbreviations). Never capitalize entire words (i.e., every letter) in titles cited in text or notes.

b. French. In prose or verse, French usage differs from English in that the following are not capitalized unless they begin a sentence or (in some cases) a line of verse: (1) the subject pronoun *je* 'I'; (2) months or days of the week; (3) names of languages and adjectives derived from proper nouns; (4) titles of people or places.

```
Un Français m'a parlé en anglais dans la place de

la Concorde.


Hier j'ai vu le docteur Maurois qui conduisait une

voiture Ford.


Le capitaine Boutillier m'a dit qu'il partait pour

Rouen le premier jeudi d'avril avec quelques amis

normands.
```

In titles of books, stories, poems, chapters, and the like,

capitalize the first word and all proper nouns. If the first word is an article, capitalize also the first noun and any preceding adjectives.

Du côté de chez Swann

Le Grand Meaulnes

La Guerre de Troie n'aura pas lieu

In titles of series and periodicals, capitalize all major words.

Nouvelle Revue des Deux Mondes

L'Ami du Peuple

c. German. In prose or verse, German usage differs from English in that the following are not capitalized unless they begin a sentence or, usually, a line of verse: (1) the subject pronoun *ich* 'I'; (2) days of the week or names of languages when used as adjectives or adverbs; (3) adjectives derived from proper nouns, except that those derived from personal names are always capitalized when they refer explicitly to the works and deeds of those persons.

Ein französischer Schriftsteller, den ich gut

kenne, arbeitet sonntags immer an seinem neuen

Buch über die platonische Liebe.

Der Staat ist eine von den bekanntesten

Platonischen Schriften.

Always capitalized in German are (1) the pronoun *Sie* 'you' and its possessive *Ihr* 'your' and their inflected forms; (2) all substantives, including any adjectives, infinitives, pronouns, prepositions, or other parts of speech used substantively; (3) adjectives derived from personal names when referring explicitly to the works and deeds of those persons (see above); (4) adjectives derived from the names of cities with the addition of the suffix -*er*; (5) ordinal numerals used in titles; (6) attributive adjectives used in titles of persons.

```
Fahren Sie mit Ihrer Frau zurück?
```

```
Ich glaube an das Gute in der Welt.
```

```
Er schreibt, nur um dem Auf und Ab der Buch-
Nachfrage zu entsprechen.
```

```
die Einsteinische Relativitätstheorie
die Berliner Luft
der Zweite Weltkrieg
Ludwig der Fromme
```

In letters and ceremonial writings, the pronouns *du* and *ihr* 'you' and their derivatives are capitalized.
   Titles follow the same usage.

```
Ein treuer Diener seines Herrn
```

```
Thomas Mann und die Grenzen des Ich
```

```
Zeitschrift für vergleichende Sprachforschung
```

d. Italian. In prose or verse, Italian usage differs from English in that the following are not capitalized unless they begin a sentence or, usually, a line of verse: (1) the subject pronoun *io* 'I'; (2) months or days of the week; (3) names of languages and adjectives derived from proper nouns; (4) titles of people or places. But centuries and other large divisions of time are capitalized.

```
Un Italiano parlava francese con uno Svizzero in

piazza di Spagna.
```

Il dottor Bruno ritornerà dall'Italia giovedì otto
agosto e io partirò il nove.

la lirica del Novecento

il Rinascimento

In all titles, the prevailing contemporary usage is to capitalize
only the first word and names of persons and places.

Dizionario letterario Bompiani

Bibliografia della critica pirandelliana

L'arte tipografica in Urbino

Collezione di classici italiani

Studi petrarcheschi

e. Portuguese. In prose or verse, Portuguese usage differs
from English in that the following are not capitalized unless
they begin a sentence or (at times) a line of verse: (1) the
subject pronoun *eu* 'I'; (2) days of the week; (3) names of the
month in Brazil (they are capitalized in Portugal); (4) adjectives derived from proper names; and (5) titles of people and
places in Portugal (they are capitalized in Brazil). As in English, points of the compass are not capitalized when indicating
direction (ao norte da América) but are capitalized when indicating regions (os americanos do Norte). Brazilian Portuguese
capitalizes nouns used to refer to abstract concepts, to institutions, or to branches of knowledge (a Igreja, a Nação, a
Matemática).

Peninsular usage:
Vi o doutor Silva na praça da República.

Brazilian usage:
O francês falava da História do Brasil na Praça

Tiradentes, utilizando o inglês.

```
Ontem eu vi o Doutor Garcia, aquele que tem um

carro Ford.
```

```
Então me disse Dona Teresa que pretendia sair para

o Recife a primeira segunda-feira de abril com

alguns amigos mineiros.
```

Capitalization of titles of books, stories, poems, chapters, and the like varies. Some writers capitalize only the first word and names of persons and places.

```
O bico da pena
```

```
O espírito das leis
```

```
Problemas da linguagem e do estilo
```

Others capitalize all major words.

```
As Viagens do Infante Dom Pedro às Quatro

    Partes do Mundo
```

```
Gabriela, Cravo e Canela
```

In titles of series, journals, and newspapers, capitalize all major words.

```
Boletim de Filologia
```

```
Revista Lusitana
```

```
Correio da Manhã
```

f. Spanish. In prose or verse, Spanish usage differs from English in that the following are not capitalized unless they begin a sentence or, sometimes, a line of verse: (1) the subject pronoun *yo* 'I'; (2) months or days of the week; (3) nouns or adjectives derived from proper nouns; (4) titles of people or places.

El francés hablaba inglés en la plaza Colón.

Ayer yo vi al doctor García, que manejaba un coche Ford.

Me dijo don Jorge que iba a salir para Sevilla el primer martes de abril con unos amigos neoyorkinos.

In titles of books, stories, poems, chapters, and the like, capitalize only the first word and names of persons and places.

Historia verdadera de la conquista de la Nueva
   España

La gloria de don Ramiro

Extremos de América

Trasmundo de Goya

Breve historia del ensayo hispanoamericano

In titles of series, journals, and newspapers, the predominant usage is to capitalize all major words.

Biblioteca de Autores Españoles

Revista de Filología Española

Fichero Bibliográfico Hispanoamericano

El Mercurio

La Nación

La Prensa

Some scholars, however, capitalize series and journal titles as book titles.

Biblioteca de autores españoles

<u>Revista de filología española</u>

g. Latin. Practice varies widely, but customary usage treats Latin prose or verse like English (except that *ego* 'I' is not capitalized). Capitalize the names of persons and places, the first word of all sentences, and the first word in lines of poetry, proverbs, epigrams, mottoes, tags, and the like.

Semper ego auditor tantum?

Numquamne reponam / Vexatus totiens rauci Theseide

Cordi?

Felix, quem faciunt aliena pericula cautum.

Timeo Danaos et dona ferentes.

Nil desperandum.

Litera scripta manet.

Quo usque tandem abutere, Catilina, patientia

nostra?

Iam primum omnium satis constat Troia capta in

ceteros saevitum esse Troianos, duobus, Aeneae

Antenorique.

In literary titles, capitalize the first word and all subsequent words except conjunctions and prepositions.

De Senectute

Liber de Senectute

De Trinitate

Tractatus de Trinitate

Initia Carminum ac Versuum Medii Aevi Posterioris

  Latinorum

The same rule applies to journals.

Medium Aevum

Medievalia et Humanistica

16 NAMES OF PERSONS

a. General remarks. Since there are exceptions to almost any rule, good judgment based on knowledge of common usage is essential in dealing with persons' names.

b. Titles. Formal titles (Mr., Mrs., Miss, Ms., Dr., Professor, etc.) are usually omitted in references to persons, living or dead. By convention, titles are associated with, or used for, certain names—for instance, the poet Henry Howard, earl of Surrey, is referred to as Surrey, not Howard. By custom, however, some titled persons are not referred to by their titles: Benjamin Disraeli, first earl of Beaconsfield, is commonly called Disraeli. A few women are traditionally known by their married names (Mme de Staël). Otherwise, women's names are treated the same as men's (Dickinson, Stein, Plath, not Miss Dickinson, Miss Stein, Miss Plath).

c. Authors' names. It is common and acceptable to use simplified names of famous authors (Vergil for Publius Vergilius Maro, Dante for Dante Alighieri). Many authors are referred to by pseudonyms, which should be treated as ordinary names.

Molière (Jean-Baptiste Poquelin)
Voltaire (François-Marie Arouet)
George Sand (Amandine-Aurore-Lucie Dupin)
George Eliot (Mary Ann Evans)
Mark Twain (Samuel Clemens)
Stendhal (Marie-Henri Beyle)
Novalis (Friedrich von Hardenberg)

In a few cases, however, surnames and pen names are virtually inseparable from initials (O. Henry, not Henry).

d. Dutch and German names. Dutch *van, van der, van den,* and German *von,* with some exceptions (especially in English contexts), are not used with the last name alone.

Droste-Hülshoff (Annette von Droste-Hülshoff)
Kleist (Heinrich von Kleist)
Vondel (Joost van den Vondel)

but

Van Gogh, Vincent
Von Braun, Wernher

German names with an umlaut (ä, ö, ü) are often alphabetized in the United States as though spelled out (ae, oe, ue). In this case, "Götz" (alphabetized as "Goetz") would precede "Gogol" in an alphabetical listing. In Germany they are most often alphabetized without regard to the umlaut.

e. French names. French *de* alone following a given name, with some exceptions, is not used with the last name alone.

Maupassant (Guy de Maupassant)
Ronsard (Pierre de Ronsard)
Scudéry (Madeleine de Scudéry)

but

De Gaulle, Charles

When the preposition *de* and the definite article are combined into a single word (*des, du*), this word is used with the last name.

Des Périers, Bonaventure
Du Bartas, Guillaume de Salluste

Otherwise, omit *de* with the last name.

La Boétie, Etienne de
La Bruyère, Jean de

A hyphen is normally used between French given names (M.-J. Chénier is Marie-Joseph Chénier, but M. R. Char is Monsieur René Char; P. J. Reynard is Père 'Father' J. Reynard).

f. Greek names. See Sec. 17g.

g. Italian names. Many Italian names of persons living before or during the Renaissance are alphabetized by the first name.

Bonvesin da la Riva
Cino da Pistoia
Dante Alighieri
Iacopone da Todi
Michelangelo Buonarroti
but
Boccaccio, Giovanni
Cellini, Benvenuto
Stampa, Gaspara

Members of historical families, however, are usually alphabetized by their last names.

Este, Beatrice d'
Medici, Lorenzo de'

In modern times, the Italian *da, de, del, della,* and *di* are used with the last name.

D'Annunzio, Gabriele
De Sanctis, Francesco
Del Buono, Oreste
Della Casa, Giovanni
Di Costanzo, Angelo

h. Spanish names. Spanish *de* is not used with the last name alone.

Madariaga (Salvador de Madariaga)
Rueda (Lope de Rueda)
Timoneda (Juan de Timoneda)

When the preposition *de* and the definite article *el* are combined into a single word (*del*), this word must be used with the last name: Del Río, Angel. Otherwise, omit *de* with the last name: Las Casas, Bartolomé de.

Spanish surnames often include both the paternal name and the maternal name, with or without the conjunction *y*. The surname of a married woman usually includes her paternal surname and the paternal surname of the husband, connected by *de*. The proper indexing of Spanish names requires the ability to distinguish between given names and surnames. Alphabetize by paternal name.

Álvarez, Miguel de los Sántos
Cervantes Saavedra, Miguel de
Díaz de Castillo, Bernal
Figuera Aymerich, Ángela
Larra y Sánchez de Castro, Mariano José
López de Ayala, Pero
Matute, Ana María
Ortega y Gasset, José
Quevedo y Villegas, Francisco Gómez de
Sinués de Marco, María del Pilar
Zayas y Sotomayor, María de

Even persons who are commonly known by the maternal portion of their surnames—Galdós, Lorca—are properly indexed under their full surnames: Benito *Pérez Galdós*, Federico *García Lorca*.

i. Oriental names. In Chinese, Japanese, Korean, and Vietnamese, surnames precede given names (Hu Shih, Wang Kuo-wei, Kim Jong Gil, Anesaki Masaharu), but Western authors should follow the known preferences of Oriental persons, even if they differ from normal practice or standard romanization (Y. R. Chao, Syngman Rhee).

17 TRANSLITERATION

The following observations are intended more to call attention to problems than to solve them. Students working on subjects that involve transliteration would do well, before the final typing, to consult with instructors about any changes in current transliteration practices. (The Univ. of Chicago Press, *A Manual of Style*, 12th ed. [1969], pp. 223–34, contains a full discussion of the special problems of transliteration.)

a. Russian, Mongolian, and Korean. For transliteration of Russian, choose the appropriate system from J. Thomas Shaw, *The Transliteration of Modern Russian for English-Language Publications* (Madison: Univ. of Wisconsin Press, 1967); for Mongolian, from Antoine Mostaert, *Dictionnaire ordos*, III (Peking, 1944; rpt. New York: Johnson Rpt., 1968), 769–809; for Korean, from McCune-Reischauer, "The Romanization of the Korean Language," *Transactions of the Korean Branch, Royal Asiatic Society,* 29 (1939), 1–55.

b. Chinese and Japanese. For Chinese, the most widely accepted system at present is still the modified Wade-Giles system given in the "List of Syllabic Headings" in the American edition of *Mathews' Chinese-English Dictionary* (Cambridge: Harvard Univ. Press, 1943), pp. xviii-xxi; in using this list, however, omit the circumflex and breve and retain the umlaut *ü*. For well-known place names, use the established forms (Yangtze, Nanking, Fukien), following the system in the *China Postal Atlas* (Nanking: Directorate General of Posts, 1933); for others, use Wade-Giles with hyphens between the elements. In general, hyphenate transcribed Chinese forms to achieve meaningful units (shih-hsüeh yen-chiu). For a comparative transcription table that includes the Yale, Wade-Giles, and *Pinyin* systems, see Fred Fangyu Wang, *Mandarin Chinese Dictionary* (South Orange, N.J.: Seton Hall Univ. Press, 1971), pp. 776–79.

For Japanese, use the romanization system of *Kenkyusha's New Japanese-English Dictionary* (Tokyo: Kenkyusha, 1974), but use an apostrophe after *n* at the end of a syllable if followed by a vowel or *y* (Ton'a, San'yo). Many scholars also prefer to represent the nasal before *b*, *p*, and *m* by *m*, rather than by *n*, as in this edition of Kenkyusha's dictionary (shimbun, sampo, shimmitsu). Use macrons over long vowels in all but well-known place names (Kyoto, Hokkaido) and anglicized Japanese words (shogun, daimyo). Use hyphens sparingly (Meiji jidai shi no shinkenkyū).

c. Indonesian, Malay, and other Southeast-Asian languages. Follow the system given in John M. Echols and Hassan Shadily, *Indonesian-English Dictionary* (2nd ed., Ithaca: Cornell Univ. Press, 1963). In the absence of a single standard form for Thai or Burmese and in view of the problem of diacritics for Vietnamese, follow any consistent, intelligible form for these languages, but avoid diacritics not in general use for other languages. For Tagalog, follow the system given in *A National Language-English Vocabulary* (4th ed., Manila: Inst. of National Language, 1950).

d. Sanskrit and Hindi. For Sanskrit, the standard system is given in A. L. Basham, *The Wonder That Was India* (3rd ed., New York: Taplinger, 1968), Appendix 10. (This coincides with most earlier systems except that the palatal sibilant is rendered as *ś* in place of *ç*). Give the stem form to nouns used in an English sentence (the *dharma* of the king; distinguish, however, *brahmā* 'the god' from *brahma* 'cosmic power'). Derivatives should be left unitalicized (the Brahmin priests, but the *brāhmana* priests). In transliteration of Hindi, the Sanskrit syllabic *r* (Kṛṣṇa) becomes *ri* (Kriṣṇa), and the following symbols in addition to those given in Basham are recommended: *q* (voiceless postvelar stop), *x* (voiceless postvelar fricative), *z* (voiced alveolar-groove fricative), *f* (voiceless labiodental fricative), and *g̣* (voiced postvelar fricative).

e. Hebrew. For transliterating Hebrew, use the Sephardi (Israeli) pronunciation and the system set forth in the *Style Manual of the U.S. Government Printing Office* (Washington, D.C.: GPO, 1973), pp. 464-69. Although Hebrew uses no capitals, in transliteration capitalize initial letters of proper names and all major words used in titles (ha-Olam); the article, however, should be capitalized if it is part of the first word in the title. Yiddish, which uses the same alphabet, should be transliterated phonetically, with special care to distinguish its spelling from that of German.

f. Languages using Arabic script. Use the transliteration tables approved by the Library of Congress and the American Library Association and published as bulletins of the United States Library of Congress, Processing Department, Cataloging Service: Bull. 49 (Nov. 1958), Arabic; Bull. 59 (July 1963), Persian; Bull. 64 (Feb. 1964), Languages of India and Pakistan, except Kashmiri, Sindhi, Pushto; Bull. 71 (July 1965), Pushto. Capitalization should be as in English except that the article *al* (and its forms) is in lowercase in all positions except when it begins a sentence (ᶜAbd al-Ḥusayn, Amīn ar-Rīḥanī). When the original publication includes a transliteration of the author's name, this should be included following the accurate transliteration, and, of course, familiar place names should be used in preference to unfamiliar transliterated forms: Tehran, Kabul, Peshawar; not Tihrān, Kābul, Pēṣhāwar.

g. Greek. For modern and classical Greek, use the transliteration tables approved by the Library of Congress and the American Library Association, printed in *A.L.A. Cataloging Rules for Author and Title Entries* (Chicago: American Library Association, 1949). In Greek books, the author's name appears on the title page in the genitive case (Hypo ["by"] Perikleous Alexandrou Argyropoulou). When a man's name is cited, the first name and most surnames are nominative (some surnames, however, are always genitive). The second, or patronymic, remains genitive because it means "son of" (Periklēs Alexandrou Argyropoulos). When a woman's name is cited, the first name is nominative, patronymic and surname both genitive (Aikaterinē Geōrgiou Koumarianou).

18

PREPARING THE MANUSCRIPT

18 TYPING AND PAPER

A fresh black ribbon and clean type are essential. Avoid type-writers with "script" or other fancy print. Type on only one side of the paper and make a copy for your files. Instructors who allow handwritten term papers also require neatness, legibility, dark ink, and use of only one side of the paper.

Use white, twenty-pound, 8½″ × 11″ paper. Do not submit any work typed on "erasable" paper, since it smudges easily and will not take corrections in ink; if you wish to use "erasable" paper because of its convenience in typing, photocopy the corrected typescript onto "plain" (not coated) paper and turn in the photocopy. Never use thin paper except for a carbon copy. (On paper for theses and dissertations, see Appendix, Sec. E.)

19 SPACING

The research paper should be double-spaced throughout, including quotations and notes. (On the placement of notes, see Sec. 30.) In a handwritten manuscript, double-spacing is indicated by skipping one ruled line. See sample pages at the conclusion of this handbook. (On spacing in the thesis or dissertation, see Appendix, Sec. E.)

20 MARGINS

Leave margins of one inch at the top, bottom, and both sides of the text. In long papers, theses, and dissertations, type chapter titles two inches from the top of the page. Double-space between lines of the title; quadruple-space (i.e., leave three blank lines) between the title and the first line of text. Indent the first word of a paragraph five spaces from the left margin; indent quotations ten spaces from the left margin (see Sec. 14). See sample pages at the conclusion of this handbook.

21 THE TITLE

A research paper does not need a title page; the title, author's name, instructor's name, course number, date, and so forth should appear instead on the first page of the paper. Skip three lines (double-space twice) between the title and the first line of text. See sample pages at the conclusion of this handbook. (For the title-page format of a dissertation, see Appendix, Sec. E.)

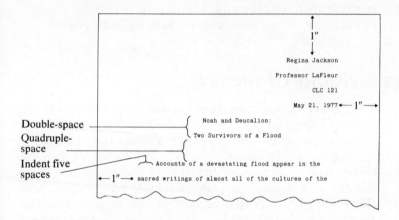

When a research paper *is* given a title page, it is not counted as the first page of the paper (dissertation title pages *are* treated as the first page; see Appendix, Sec. D).

The title is never put in quotation marks, underlined, or capitalized in full. (For capitalization, see Sec. 15.) Words are underlined in the title only if they would also be underlined in the text (see Sec. 10h).

```
Local Television Coverage of Recent International

   News Events

The Attitude toward Violence in Anthony Burgess' A

   Clockwork Orange
```

```
Vergil and the Locus Amoenus Tradition in Latin

   Literature

The Use of the Noun Chevisaunce in Chaucer and

   Spenser
```

A period should not be used after titles or any centered headings, including Roman numerals used alone as section headings (see Sec. 22). The title ordinarily does not carry a symbol or number referring to a note. (Editors will occasionally violate this practice to cite the source of the work being printed.)

22 DIVISIONS OF THE TEXT

Term papers rarely have formal divisions. Related groups of paragraphs may be separated from the preceding and following groups of paragraphs by skipping three lines (i.e., by double-spacing twice). In longer papers (or in chapters of dissertations), unified sections of thought are sometimes numbered (usually with Roman numerals); a subtitle may also be added (II. From 1965 to 1971). The number and the subtitle appear four lines below the last line of the previous section and are either centered on the page or typed flush with the left margin. The first paragraph of the new section begins four lines below the subtitle. (See Appendix, Sec. C, for divisions of the text in dissertations.)

23 TABLES AND ILLUSTRATIONS

Illustrative material should be placed as close as possible to the part of the text that it illustrates. Tables are usually labeled as "tables," given Arabic numerals, and captioned; both label and caption should be completely in capital letters. Place the statement of the source of a table and any notes to the table immediately below the table; do not number the notes in the same series as the notes to the text (common practice is to use lowercase letters for notes to tables). Double-space throughout, ruling as needed.

TABLE 1

INSTITUTIONS OF HIGHER EDUCATION IN THE UNITED STATES

Type of institution	Public	Private	Total
Doctoral-granting universities	108	65	173
Comprehensive colleges and universities	308	145	453
Liberal arts colleges	23	691	719
Two-year institutions	805	256	1,061
Specialized institutions[a]	64	357	421
Total	1,313	1,514	2,827

Source: ADE Bulletin, No. 45 (May 1975), p. 1.

[a] This group consists mainly of seminaries and medical, engineering, and law schools.

Other types of illustrative material—photographs, maps, line drawings, graphs, charts, and so forth—should be labeled as "figures" (often abbreviated), assigned Arabic numbers, and given titles or captions (Fig. 1. Cousin, *Eva Prima Pandora*, Louvre). In a dissertation, the List of Illustrations or List of Tables immediately follows the Table of Contents (see Appendix, Sec. C).

24 PAGINATION

Number pages consecutively throughout the manuscript in the upper right-hand corner. (Typing your name and course number beneath the page number is good insurance against misplaced pages.) Do not punctuate page numbers by adding periods, hyphens, or other characters. In a research paper, the first page of the text, the first page of endnotes, and the first page of the bibliography often do not have numbers appearing on the page, although such pages are counted in the total pagination of the work. (For the placement of the title in the research paper, see Sec. 21 and the sample pages at the conclusion of this handbook.) It is, therefore, the second page of the text that receives the first number.

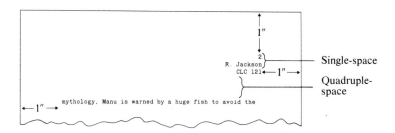

On paginating the dissertation, see Appendix, Sec. D.

25 CORRECTIONS AND INSERTIONS

Proofread and correct the research paper or dissertation carefully before submitting it. If permitted by the instructor, brief corrections on a research paper may be typed or written legibly in ink directly above the line involved. Do not use the margins or write below the line. If the corrections on any one page are substantial, retype the page. Dissertations should be free of typing errors.

26 BINDING

Research papers should be handed in as scholars submit manuscripts to publishers, secured only by a paper clip. (On binding the dissertation, see Appendix, Sec. E.)

DOCUMENTATION

27 GENERAL REMARKS

Although sources of quotations and authorities for statements of fact or opinion must be cited in a scholarly study, such citations should be kept as concise as clarity and accuracy permit. Notes may include information or commentary to support the text, but never to rival or overshadow it. References are usually placed in endnotes, at the end of the paper or chapter, or in footnotes, at the bottom of the page (see Sec. 30), but brief references may be placed in parentheses, within the text itself (see Secs. 37b and 39). The test should be whether or not the reference interferes with ease in reading. Remember that a note number, which teases the reader to look at the end of the paper or at the bottom of the page,[1] may be more disruptive than a simple reference in the text, such as (II, 241), (III.ii.21), or (p. 72). To avoid large numbers of very short notes, consolidate references as often as possible without sacrificing clarity (see Sec. 36). Except when presenting incomplete quotations introduced by three spaced periods, begin notes with capitals and end with periods. Notes are intended to be read like sentences, without internal full stops— hence the enclosure of place of publication, publisher, and date of publication within parentheses, whereas in bibliographies these items are set off by periods.

28 NOTE LOGIC

The conventions of documentation are a means to an end: to lend authority and credibility to your work and to enable the reader to locate sources with ease. Provide a note only where there is reason. It is rarely necessary, for example, to give references for proverbs ("You can't judge a book by its cover"), familiar quotations ("We shall overcome"), or common knowledge ("Washington was the first President of the United States"); to give line references for short poems (e.g.,

---

[1] Like this. And suppose you had found only "Ibid."

sonnets); to spell out the full names of familiar authors (Shake-speare, Dante, Cervantes); or to give page references to works arranged alphabetically (e.g., dictionaries). To include such information in citations is to forget the reader and think only of the machinery of scholarship. Information given in the text need not be repeated in a note (see Sec. 32b). Successive quotations in one paragraph may usually be documented in a single note, and "covering notes" may be used to acknowl-edge general sources, thereby avoiding a series of citations: Howarth, p. xii. I follow throughout Howarth's account of the sources.

On the other hand, do not give too little information. In references to prose classics of which many editions are avail-able, it is helpful to provide more information than just the page number of the edition used—for example, p. 271 (Bk. IV, Ch. ii) *or* Bk. IV, Ch. ii (p. 271). In citing sources that do not state complete information (author, title, or full publication information), supply within square brackets what information you know or can ascertain (see sample notes 58 and 64 in Secs. 32r and 32t).

29 NOTE NUMBERS

Notes should be numbered consecutively, starting from 1, throughout a research paper or a chapter of a thesis or disserta-tion unless a special section—such as an annotated text or a numerical table (see Sec. 23)—requires a separate series. Do not number notes by individual pages or use asterisks or other symbols. Use Arabic numbers without periods, parentheses, or slashes. Note numbers are "superior figures"; in the text type them slightly above the line. They should be placed *after* all punctuation (including parentheses) except a dash. Avoid interrupting the flow of thought of a sentence with note num-bers. Place the note number at the end of an appropriate syntactical unit that is as near as possible to the material quoted or referred to. The note number should always come after, but not necessarily immediately after, a paraphrase or direct quotation.

In his <u>Autobiography</u>, Benjamin Franklin states that

he prepared a list of "twelve virtues," and later

added a thirteenth.[1]

is preferable to

In his <u>Autobiography</u>,[1] Benjamin Franklin

states. . . .

Wilson, Chambers, and Lewis support this view.[1]

is preferable to

Wilson,[1] Chambers,[2] and Lewis[3] support this

view.

Never place the note number immediately after the author's name, the introductory verb, or the colon preceding a paraphrase or quotation.

Wrong:

Ernst Rose[1] writes, "The highly spiritual view of

the world presented in <u>Siddhartha</u> exercised its

appeal on West and East alike."

Wrong:

Ernst Rose writes,[1] "The highly spiritual view of

the world presented in <u>Siddhartha</u> exercised its

appeal on West and East alike."

Right:

Ernst Rose writes, "The highly spiritual view of

the world presented in <u>Siddhartha</u> exercised its

appeal on West and East alike."[1]

Note (see Sec. 30 on the placement of notes):

    [1] <u>Faith from the Abyss: Hermann Hesse's Way</u>

<u>from Romanticism to Modernity</u> (New York: New York Univ. Press, 1965), p. 74.

Verify both note numbers and the references themselves before submitting a paper.

30 ENDNOTES AND FOOTNOTES

In research papers, give all notes as endnotes. Endnotes, as their name implies, appear at the conclusion of the text. They should begin on a new page (often without a number), the title Notes appearing two inches from the top of the page (on margins and pagination, see, respectively, Secs. 20 and 24). Skip three lines (i.e., double-space twice) below the title, indent five spaces, and begin the first line of the first note. Type the note number without punctuation slightly above the line, skip a space, and begin the reference. Type the notes consecutively, with double-spacing, on as many pages as necessary. All pages of endnotes after the first are numbered.

Endnotes (notes grouped together at the end of the work):

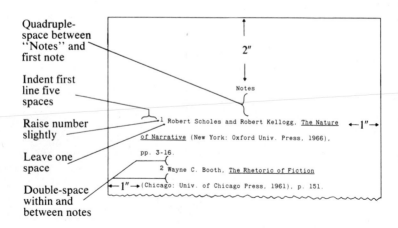

See sample pages at the conclusion of this handbook.

In dissertations, notes usually appear at the bottom of the page. Separate the first footnote on any page from the last line of the text by skipping three lines (double-spacing twice). Single-space all footnotes, double-spacing between them. (On margins, see Sec. 20.)

Footnotes (notes appearing at the bottom of the relevant page):

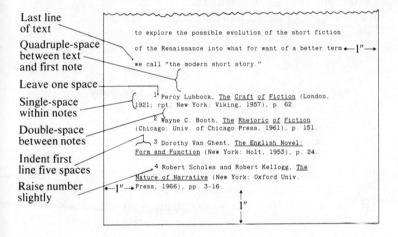

Last line of text	to explore the possible evolution of the short fiction
Quadruple-space between text and first note	of the Renaissance into what for want of a better term ◄—1″—►
	we call "the modern short story."
Leave one space	
Single-space within notes	1 Percy Lubbock, *The Craft of Fiction* (London, 1921; rpt. New York: Viking, 1957), p. 62.
	2 Wayne C. Booth, *The Rhetoric of Fiction* (Chicago: Univ. of Chicago Press, 1961), p. 151.
Double-space between notes	3 Dorothy Van Ghent, *The English Novel: Form and Function* (New York: Holt, 1953), p. 24.
Indent first line five spaces	4 Robert Scholes and Robert Kellogg, *The Nature of Narrative* (New York: Oxford Univ.
Raise number slightly	◄—1″—► Press, 1966), pp. 3-16.
	1″

If the length of a note requires that it be continued on the following page, type a solid line across the new page one full line below the last line of the text, double-space twice, and continue the note. Footnotes pertaining to this new page should immediately follow the completion of the note continued from the previous page.

31 FIRST NOTE REFERENCES FOR PUBLISHED BOOKS: STANDARD FORM

For examples of the various recommendations set forth in this section, see Sec. 32. (On abridging notes because of material given in the text, see Sec. 32b.) In notes, the following order should be used (see Sec. 41 for the form of a listing in a bibliography).

a. Name(s) of author(s) in normal order (first name first, etc.), followed by a comma. Give the names in their fullest, or at least in their most usual, form; this practice may save the reader many minutes of search in a library catalog ("Carleton Brown" is more helpful than merely "C. Brown"). Common sense will have to guide the author in applying this recommendation; "Thomas Stearns Eliot" or "Herbert M. McLuhan" instead of the more familiar "T. S. Eliot" and "H. Marshall McLuhan" might confuse the reader. Square brackets may be used to indicate parts of a name not found in the work cited—for example, C[live] S[taples] Lewis. Occasionally, it is more appropriate to cite the name of an editor or translator first (see Sec. 31d). On citing anonymous works, see Sec. 32e.

b. Title of the chapter or part of the book cited, enclosed in quotation marks (not underlined), followed by a comma inside the final quotation marks. This detail is necessary only in reference to pieces within anthologies and collections of works. Words referring to untitled parts of a book—Introduction, Preface—are capitalized but are not put in quotation marks or underlined (see sample note 39 in Sec. 32l). When citing from an anthology a work originally published separately (such as a novel), underline the title of such a work (see sample note 23 in Sec. 32h).

c. Title of the work, underlined, followed by a comma unless the next detail is enclosed within parentheses or unless the title has its own punctuation (e.g., a question mark). Unusually long titles may be abbreviated; but the first few words should always be cited verbatim, and any later omissions *within* the portion cited should be indicated by three spaced periods (. . .). (On ellipsis within quotations, see Sec. 14d.) Always take the title from the title page, not from the cover or the title printed at the top of each page; disregard any unusual typographical characteristics, such as all capital letters or uncommon use of lowercase letters, unless you know them to reflect the author's wishes (CONCEPTS OF CRITICISM should be capitalized as *Concepts of Criticism*; Turner's early sketchbooks as *Turner's Early Sketchbooks*; e. e. cummings' i: six nonlectures may be left in lowercase). If there is a subtitle, underline it and separate it from the title by a colon, which is also underlined. The word "in" (not underlined) may precede the title of the work if a chapter or a part of the book is being cited.

d. Name(s) of editor(s), translator(s), and compiler(s) in normal order, preceded by "ed.," "trans.," or "comp." (without parentheses) and followed by a comma unless the next detail is enclosed in parentheses. If the actual editing, translating, or compiling itself, rather than the text, is under discussion, give the name(s) of the editor(s), translator(s), or compiler(s) first in your reference (followed by a comma, followed by "ed.," "trans.," or "comp." and another comma) and the author's name after the title, preceded by a comma and the word "by" (see sample notes 38 and 42 in Secs. 32l and 32m).

e. Edition used, whenever it is not the first, designated by an Arabic numeral (e.g., 4th ed.), followed by a comma unless the next detail is enclosed in parentheses. Unless you are concerned with an author's changes of opinion or with differences in text, use the latest revised edition or inform the reader of your inability to do so. In a period of competitive reprinting, it is especially important to distinguish the *original date* and *edition* from the *reprint* you may happen to be using. (On citing reprints, see Sec. 32k.) For example, all the following information would be necessary to avoid confusion: Emile Mâle, *The Gothic Image: Religious Art of the Thirteenth Century*, trans. Dora Nussey from 3rd French ed. (1913; rpt. New York: Harper, 1973), p. 90. Without the inclusion of "1913" and "rpt.," this reference to a useful paperback version of Mâle's classic study would make *The Gothic Image* appear to be a recent work.

f. The series (e.g., Univ. of California Publications in Modern Philology), not underlined and not in quotation marks, followed by a comma, followed by an Arabic numeral designating the number of this work in the series (e.g., Vol. 7, No. 7, or simply 7 as given on the title page or half-title page), followed by a comma unless the next detail is enclosed in parentheses (see sample notes 31-33 in Sec. 32j).

g. The number of volumes with this particular title, if more than one (e.g., 3 vols.) and if the information is pertinent. It is usually not pertinent when the reference is to a specific passage rather than to the work as a whole (see Sec. 32f).

h. Place of publication, publisher, and date of publication, all within parentheses. A colon follows the place, a comma follows the publisher, and the closing parenthesis follows the date: (Cleveland: Western Reserve Univ. Press, 1967).

The place of publication should be taken from the title page or copyright page (i.e., the reverse of the title page). If several cities are listed for the publisher, list only one, preferably the one in which the book originated or, if that is not known, a major city. Specify enough detail to avoid ambiguity (York, Pa.; Portland, Me.; Portland, Ore.); if the city is not well known, include the state or country as well (Englewood Cliffs, N.J.). If no place of publication is given, indicate by writing "n.p." for "no place" (see Sec. 32t).

An appropriately shortened form of the name of the publisher may be used. Blaisdell Publishing Co., George Braziller, Inc., and Harcourt Brace Jovanovich may be safely identified in notes and bibliography as Blaisdell, Braziller, and Harcourt, respectively. W. Heffer & Sons, Ltd., and Librairie Larousse may be recognized as Heffer and Larousse, respectively. A university press must always be so designated, since the university may publish independently of its press (see sample notes 1 and 48 in Secs. 32b and 32p). In citing a work published under a publisher's special imprint, add the publisher's name after a hyphen (e.g., Anchor-Doubleday). The name of the publisher may be omitted for works published prior to 1900. If no publisher is listed, indicate by writing "n.p." ("no publisher"). Although this is also the abbreviation for "no place," confusion is avoided by noting on which side of the colon the "n.p." appears (see Sec. 32t). If a work is privately printed, so indicate by writing "privately printed" (see sample note 47 in Sec. 32o).

The date of publication appears on the title page or the copyright page. If the copyright page indicates that the work has gone through several impressions or printings by the same publisher—printings undifferentiated in any way (including page numbers) from the first edition—use the original publication date (see sample note 3 in Sec. 32b). In citing a new or revised edition, give the date of that edition (not the original edition); in citing a reprint by a different publisher, give the dates of both the original edition and the reprint (see sample notes in Sec. 32k). If no date of publication is recorded on the title page, copyright page, or (particularly for books published outside the United States) in the colophon at the back of the book, use the latest date of copyright, if given; otherwise, write "n.d." (see Sec. 32t) or supply in square brackets an approximate date (a question mark may be added).

i. Volume number, if one of two or more, in capital Roman numerals, preceded and followed by a comma. If it is necessary to give the date of a single volume of a multivolume work published over a number of years, indicate the volume number *before* the publication information (see sample note 17 in Sec. 32f). Use the volume number alone (without "Vol.") if page numbers follow (III, 248-51).

j. Page number(s) in Arabic numerals (unless the original has Roman numerals), preceded by a comma, followed by a period unless an additional reference is required (p. 47, n. 3. *or* p. 47, col. 2.). If the source of a quotation is being given, probably only a page or two will be indicated; but, if the reader is being directed to a discussion of some question, numerous pages may be cited. See Sec. 11a for writing page numbers over three digits and Sec. 11d for inclusive page numbers.

Omit "Vol." and "p." or "pp." when volume and page numbers are both given: III, 142. But "Vol." and "p." or "pp." must be included when the volume number applies to the general title of the multivolume work and not to the title of the individual volume being cited (see sample notes 18 and 19 in Secs. 32f and 32g). If there is no pagination, indicate "n. pag." (see Sec. 32t). If a book lacks page numbers but has signatures, indicate "sig." rather than "p." (see Sec. 32v); if it numbers columns instead of pages, indicate "col." rather than "p." (On omission of volume and page numbers for reference works, see Sec. 32i.)

32 FIRST NOTE REFERENCES FOR PUBLISHED BOOKS: SAMPLE NOTES

a. General remarks. Following are examples of the various recommendations in Sec. 31. For bibliographical citations that parallel the sample notes in each of these lettered subsections, see the corresponding lettered subsection of Sec. 42.

b. A book with a single author. This is the simplest and probably the most widely used form of reference. It follows the general pattern outlined in Sec. 31. (Note that in this and in all subsequent examples double-spacing is used, as it would be for endnotes; for spacing in dissertations, see Appendix, Sec. E.)

> [1] Northrop Frye, <u>Anatomy of Criticism: Four Essays</u> (Princeton: Princeton Univ. Press, 1957), p. 52.

The subtitle may be omitted in endnotes and footnotes, but it must be included in a bibliographical listing. The subtitle is separated from the title by a colon, which, like all other punctuation marks within a title, is underlined. (If the author's name, with or without the title, has been given in the text, the author's name may be omitted in the note. The omission of both the author and the title might prove confusing.)

Text:

In the <u>Anatomy of Criticism</u>, Northrop Frye expounds his influential "theory of modes."[2]

Note:

> [2] <u>Anatomy of Criticism</u> (Princeton: Princeton Univ. Press, 1957), pp. 33-67.

In the following, the choice of date could have been a problem, since the copyright page reads "© 1961. Published 1961. First text impression 1963. Fifth impression 1965." Although the fifth impression is the one being used, the date of publication is cited as 1961:

³ Wayne C. Booth, <u>The Rhetoric of Fiction</u>

(Chicago: Univ. of Chicago Press, 1961), pp. 73-74.

(On citing other editions, see Sec. 31e.)
  Following are notes to books published in other countries:

⁴ Heinrich Meyer, <u>Goethe: Das Leben im Werk</u>

(Stuttgart: Günther, 1967), pp. 101-11.

⁵ Dharma P. Sarin, <u>The Influence of Political</u>
<u>Movements on Hindi Literature, 1906-1947</u>
(Chandigarh: Punjab Univ. Publications Bureau,
1968), p. 58.

⁶ Michael Gelfand, <u>African Background: The</u>
<u>Traditional Culture of the Shona-Speaking People</u>
(Cape Town: Juta, 1965), p. 61.

c. A book with two or more authors. Cite all authors as they appear on the title page—not necessarily in alphabetical order.

⁷ Oscar Cargill, William Charvat, and Donald
D. Walsh, <u>The Publication of Academic Writing</u> (New
York: MLA, 1966), p. 8.

⁸ René Wellek and Austin Warren, <u>Theory of</u>
<u>Literature</u>, 3rd ed. (New York: Harcourt, 1962),
p. 289.

Even if the authors have the same last name, state each author's name as it appears on the title page. If there are more than three authors, one name followed by "et al." or "and others," with no comma in between, may be used.

⁹ Barbara B. Burn et al., <u>Higher Education in Nine Countries: A Comparative Study of Colleges and Universities Abroad</u> (New York: McGraw-Hill, 1971), p. 125.

d. A book with a corporate author may be cited in both notes and bibliography either by its corporate author or by its title followed by a comma, the word "by," and the name of the corporate author. (On government publications, see Sec. 32r.)

¹⁰ President's Commission on Higher Education, <u>Higher Education for American Democracy</u> (Washington, D.C.: GPO, 1947), I, 26.
or
¹¹ <u>Higher Education for American Democracy</u>, by the President's Commission on Higher Education (Washington, D.C.: GPO, 1947), I, 26.

In the following example the corporate author is clear from the title and need not be stated separately:

¹² <u>Report of the Commission on the Humanities</u> (New York: American Council of Learned Societies, 1964), p. 139.

To place "Commission on the Humanities" before the title or "by the Commission on the Humanities" after the title would be redundant. In this book, as in many similar publications, no publisher is indicated on the title page or elsewhere; but the names of the American Council of Learned Societies, the Council of Graduate Schools, and the United Chapters of Phi Beta Kappa are on the cover and sign the sponsor's Foreword. Copies, it is further indicated, may be ordered from the American Council. Therefore, for all but bibliographical essays, the citation above is adequate.

e. An anonymous book. If the author of a work is unknown, cite it by title in both notes and bibliography, without using either "Anonymous" or "Anon."

13 <u>Literary Market Place: The Directory of</u> <u>American Book Publishing</u>, 1976-77 ed. (New York: Bowker, 1976), p. 129.

14 <u>The World of Learning 1975-76</u>, 26th ed. (London: Europa, 1975), I, 734.

If you are able to determine the name(s) of the author(s) of a book published anonymously, give the name(s) within square brackets.

f. A work in several volumes or parts. When drawing attention to an entire multivolume work, use the following form:

15 See William R. Parker, <u>Milton: A Biography</u>, 2 vols. (Oxford: Clarendon, 1968).

But if citing only one volume of a multivolume work, use the following:

16 David Daiches, <u>A Critical History of</u> <u>English Literature</u>, 2nd ed. (New York: Ronald, 1970), II, 776-77.

If the volumes of a work have been published in different years, the volume number *precedes* the publishing information. The first two volumes of the following work were published in 1955, the second two in 1965:

17 René Wellek, <u>A History of Modern Criticism, 1750-1950</u>, III (New Haven: Yale Univ. Press, 1965), 1-32.

If the individual volumes of a multivolume work have separate titles, use the following form:

18 Winston S. Churchill, <u>The Age of Revolution</u>, Vol. III of <u>A History of the English-Speaking Peoples</u> (New York: Dodd, Mead, 1957), pp. 131-32.

g. A work in a collection of pieces all by the same author. The title of the part of the book is placed in quotation marks, followed by a comma (inside the final quotation mark), the word "in," and the title of the book underlined. (On citing a preface or introduction or a part originally published as a book, see Secs. 31b and 32l.)

19 Antoine Adam, "Descartes," in <u>L'Epoque d'Henri IV et de Louis XIII</u>, Vol. I of <u>Histoire de la littérature française au XVIIe siècle</u> (Paris: Domat, 1948), pp. 319-29.

20 Kemp Malone, "Etymologies for <u>Hamlet</u>," in his <u>Studies in Heroic Legend and in Current Speech</u>, ed. S. Einarsson and N. E. Eliason (Copenhagen: Rosenkilde and Bagger, 1959), pp. 204-25.

In sample note 20, the word "his" was added to assure the reader, who may have been misled by the title and the listing of editors, that the book is indeed the work of one author.

h. A work in a collection of pieces by different authors.
The following illustrate the standard forms for citing pieces in an anthology, casebook, or collection of essays:

21 Richard Wright, "Bright and Morning Star," in <u>Short Stories: A Critical Anthology</u>, ed. Ensaf Thune and Ruth Prigozy (New York: Macmillan, 1973), pp. 387-88.

22 Flannery O'Connor, "Everything That Rises Must Converge," in <u>Mirrors: An Introduction to Literature</u>, ed. John R. Knott, Jr., and Christopher R. Reaske, 2nd ed. (San Francisco: Canfield, 1975), p. 66.

23 Miguel de Unamuno y Jugo, <u>Abel Sanchez</u>, trans. Anthony Kerrigan, in <u>Eleven Modern Short Novels</u>, ed. Leo Hamalian and Edmond L. Volpe, 2nd ed. (New York: Putnam, 1970), pp. 342-44.

On citing translations, see Sec. 32m.

Collections of important essays and articles are becoming increasingly convenient in research; the conscientious writer, however, informs the reader of the original date and source of the piece collected. (The original title should also be given if, as is often true, the piece appears untitled or under a different title in the collection.)

24 Marie Padgett Hamilton, "The Meaning of

the Middle English <u>Pearl</u>," <u>PMLA</u>, 70 (1955), 805-24;

rpt. in <u>Middle English Survey: Critical Essays</u>,

ed. Edward Vasta (Notre Dame, Ind.: Univ. of Notre

Dame Press, 1965), p. 117.

[25] C. S. Lewis, "The Anthropological

Approach," in <u>English and Medieval Studies</u>

<u>Presented to J. R. R. Tolkien on the Occasion of His</u>

<u>Seventieth Birthday</u>, ed. Norman Davis and C. L.

Wrenn (London: Allen and Unwin, 1962), pp. 219-23;

rpt. "View Points: C. S. Lewis," in <u>Twentieth</u>

<u>Century Interpretations of</u> Sir Gawain and the Green

Knight, ed. Denton Fox (Englewood Cliffs, N.J.:

Prentice-Hall, 1968), pp. 100-01.

i. Articles in reference works. An encyclopedia article is cited as a work in a collection, but without the ''in'' preceding the title, without an editor's name, and, especially if it is a well-known encyclopedia, without publication information except for edition (if given) and year. If the article is signed, the author is cited first; if unsigned, the title comes first. (Often articles in reference books are signed with initials that are identified in the index or in another volume.) In a work that is alphabetically arranged, volume and page number may also be omitted; volume and page number, however, must be given if the citation is to only one page of a multipage article.

[26] "Mandarin," <u>Encyclopedia Americana</u>, 1976

ed.

[27] Luciano Chiappini, "Este, House of," <u>New</u>

<u>Encyclopaedia Britannica: Macropaedia</u>, 1974 ed.

A similar form is used for annuals, yearbooks, and many other reference books.

28 "Mead, Margaret," Who's Who of American Women, 8th ed. (1974-75).

29 John C. French, "Norris, Benjamin Franklin," DAB (1934).

30 William Cosmo Monkhouse, "Reynolds, Sir Joshua," DNB (1896).

j. A work in a series. These examples follow the procedures described in Sec. 31f.

31 Ruth C. Wallerstein, Richard Crashaw: A Study in Style and Poetic Development, Univ. of Wisconsin Studies in Lang. and Lit., No. 37 (Madison: Univ. of Wisconsin Press, 1935), p. 52.

32 Sigfrid Hoefert, Das Drama des Naturalismus, Sammlung Metzler, 75 (Stuttgart: Metzler, 1968), p. 103.

33 John H. Fisher, "The Progress of Research in Medieval English Literature in the United States of America," English Studies Today, 4th ser., ed. Ilva Cellini and Giorgio Melchiori (Rome: Edizioni di Storia e Letteratura, 1966), pp. 33-34.

k. A modern reprint of an older edition. In citing reprints, give the date of the original edition. If the original work appeared in a different country, include the original place of publication as well.

³⁴ John Livingston Lowes, <u>The Road to Xanadu:
A Study in the Ways of the Imagination</u>, 2nd ed.
(1930; rpt. New York: Vintage-Knopf, 1959), p. 231.

³⁵ René Bray, <u>La Formation de la doctrine
classique en France</u> (1927; rpt. Paris: Nizet,
1966), p. 301.

³⁶ Basil Willey, <u>The Eighteenth Century
Background</u> (London, 1940; rpt. Boston: Beacon,
1961), p. 43.

I. An edition should be cited as follows:

³⁷ W. D. Howells, <u>A Hazard of New Fortunes</u>,
ed. David J. Nordloh et al. (Bloomington: Indiana
Univ. Press, 1976), p. 217.

(For the bibliographical listing of this work, which is the sixteenth volume of *A Selected Edition of W. D. Howells,* see Sec. 42l.)

If the work of the editor is being discussed or cited, the editor's name should come first.

³⁸ Charlton Hinman, ed., <u>The First Folio of
Shakespeare: The Norton Facsimile</u> (New York:
Norton, 1968), p. ix.

In citing an introduction, preface, foreword, or afterword written by neither the author nor the editor, give the writer's name followed by a comma and Introd., Pref., Foreword, or Afterword, with initial capital letters but without quotation marks. Then list the title of the book preceded by a comma, and the name of the author, preceded by a comma and the word "by." The writer of a preface or introduction is not necessarily the editor of the book, and no person associated with a text should be labeled "editor" unless so identified on the title page. It is common practice for a publisher to commission a scholar to write an introduction to a standard novel and to publish that introduction with a resetting of an edition of the work. In citing such an introduction, use the following form:

39 Henry Nash Smith, Introd., The Prairie: A Tale, by James Fenimore Cooper (New York: Holt, 1950), p. xx.

In citing the text of this edition, use the following form (see Sec. 28 on the inclusion of the chapter number):

40 James Fenimore Cooper, The Prairie: A Tale, introd. Henry Nash Smith (New York: Holt, 1950), Ch. xxiii (p. 281).

For subsequent reference to an edition, see Sec. 37b.

m. A translation should be cited as follows:

41 Feodor Dostoevsky, Crime and Punishment, trans. Jessie Coulson, ed. George Gibian (New York: Norton, 1964), p. 157.

If the work of the translator is being discussed or cited, his or her name comes first.

⁴² Jessie Coulson, trans., <u>Crime and Punishment</u>, by Feodor Dostoevsky, ed. George Gibian (New York: Norton, 1964), p. 157.

⁴³ George C. Schoolfield, trans., <u>The German Lyric of the Baroque in English Translation</u>, Univ. of North Carolina Studies in Germanic Langs. and Lits., 29 (Chapel Hill: Univ. of North Carolina Press, 1961), p. 147.

⁴⁴ Alfonso Sastre, <u>Sad Are the Eyes of William Tell</u>, trans. Leonard C. Pronko, in <u>The New Wave Spanish Drama</u>, ed. George E. Wellwarth (New York: New York Univ. Press, 1970), p. 309.

n. An unpublished dissertation. The title should be placed in quotation marks, not underlined. Abbreviate "dissertation" as "Diss." No commas are placed between "Diss." and the name of the degree-granting university or between the university and the date of completion. The name of the university may be shortened, as long as it remains unambiguous (e.g., "Johns Hopkins" is clear, but "New York" could refer to a number of institutions).

⁴⁵ Eric L. Gans, "The Discovery of Illusion: Flaubert's Early Works, 1835-1837," Diss. Johns Hopkins 1967, p. 34.

For a reference to a dissertation abstract published in *Dissertation Abstracts* or *Dissertation Abstracts International*, see Sec. 34m.

o. A published dissertation is treated as a book except for the inclusion of pertinent dissertation information.

⁴⁶ Per Nykrog, Les Fabliaux: Etude d'histoire littéraire et de stylistique médiévale, Diss. Aarhus 1956 (Copenhagen: Munksgaard, 1957), p. 68.

⁴⁷ Karl Georg Wendriner, Der Einfluss von Goethes Wilhelm Meister auf das Drama der Romantiker, Diss. Bonn 1907 (Leipzig: privately printed, 1907), p. 52.

p. The published proceedings of a conference usually appear in a note beginning with the title of the meeting, followed by pertinent information regarding the conference and the publication of its proceedings.

⁴⁸ Humanistic Scholarship in America, Proc. of a Conference on the Princeton Studies in the Humanities, 5-6 Nov. 1965 (Princeton: Princeton Univ., 1966).

q. A pamphlet is generally cited as a book would be.

⁴⁹ Modern Language Association of America, A Guide for Job Candidates and Department Chairmen in English and Foreign Languages, rev. ed. (New York: MLA, 1975), p. 26.

r. Government publications are numerous, and their citation in notes and bibliography can be a complicated matter. In general, in citing a government document, indicate the agency first. (If, however, the name of an author is known, it may be given first or, if the agency is listed first, placed after the title and preceded by a comma and the word "by"; see sample notes 54 and 55.) The name of the agency may be abbreviated if the context makes it clear.

```
U.S. Cong., Senate

U.S. Cong., House

U.S. Dept. of Health, Education, and Welfare

Calif. Dept. of Industrial Relations

Chicago Board of Trade
```

The title of the publication (underlined) should follow immediately. In citing a Congressional document other than the *Congressional Record* (which requires only date and page number), include such information as the number and session of Congress, the house (S. or H.R.), and the type and number of publication. Types of Congressional publications include bills (S. 33; H.R. 77), resolutions (S. Res. 20; H. Res. 50), reports (S. Rept. 9; H. Rept. 142), and documents (S. Doc. 333; H. Doc. 222). The usual publishing information comes next (i.e., place, publisher, date). Most federal publications, regardless of the branch of government, are published by the Government Printing Office (GPO) in Washington, D.C.; its British counterpart is Her Majesty's Stationery Office (HMSO) in London. Since documents of the United Nations and most local governments do not issue from a central office, give full publishing information as it appears on the title page.

```
    50 Cong. Rec., 7 Feb. 1973, pp. 3831-51.
or
    51 Cong. Rec., Feb. 7, 1973, pp. 3831-51.

    52 U.S. Bureau of Labor Statistics,
Productivity (Washington, D.C.: GPO, 1958), p. 10.

    53 U.S. Cong., Joint Committee on the
Investigation of the Pearl Harbor Attack,
```

Hearings, 79th Cong., 1st and 2nd sess.

(Washington, D.C.: GPO, 1946), I, 25.

[54] U.S. Cong., House, Memphis Riots and

Massacres, by E. B. Washburne, 39th Cong.,

2nd sess., H. Rept. 101 (1866; rpt. New York:

Arno, 1969), p. 14.

or

[55] E. B. Washburne, Memphis Riots and

Massacres, U.S. 39th Cong., 2nd sess., H. Rept.

101 (1866; rpt. New York: Arno, 1969), p. 14.

[56] U.S. Cong., Senate, Special Committee

to Investigate Organized Crime in Interstate

Commerce, Report on Crime Investigation,

82nd Cong., 1st sess., S. Rept. 141

(Washington, D.C.: GPO, 1951), pp. 1-5.

[57] New York State, Committee on State

Prisons, Investigation of the New York State

Prisons (1883; rpt. New York: Arno, 1974),

p. 32.

[58] New York City, Knapp Commission, The

Knapp Commission Report on Police Corruption

(New York: Braziller, [1973?]), pp. 23-24.

[59] Great Britain, Ministry of Defence,

Author and Subject Catalogues of the Naval

Library, Ministry of Defence (London: HMSO, 1967),

IV, 135.

[60] United Nations, Economic Commission for Africa, <u>Industrial Growth in Africa</u> (New York: United Nations, 1963), pp. 32-33.

s. Legal references offer an even more elaborate and complicated system of annotation than government publications. The indispensable guide for legal work is *A Uniform System of Citation*, 12th ed. (Cambridge: Harvard Law Review Association, 1976). In general, laws, acts, and similar documents are not italicized in either text or notes (Declaration of Independence, Constitution of the United States, Taft-Hartley Act). In such citations, one refers to sections rather than pages; the year number should be added if relevant. Although lawyers and legal scholars adopt many abbreviations in their citations, use only familiar abbreviations when writing for a more general audience.

[61] U.S. Const., art. I, sec. 1.

[62] 15 U.S. Code, sec. 78j(b) (1964).

(Note that in references to the United States Code, often abbreviated as U.S.C., the title number must be included: 12 U.S.C., 15 U.S.C., etc.) Names of law cases are both abbreviated and shortened (Brown v. Board of Ed. *for* Brown vs. Board of Education of Topeka, Kansas), but the first important word of each party is always spelled out. Unlike laws, names of cases are always italicized in text; in notes, they are not. The information required in citing a case includes the name of the first plaintiff and first defendant; the volume, name, and page (in that order) of the law report cited; the name of the court that decided the case; and the year in which it was decided. Once again, considerable abbreviation is the norm.

[63] Stevens v. National Broadcasting Co., 148 U.S.P.Q. 755 (Cal. Super. Ct. 1966).

This note cites page 755 of volume 148 of the *United States*

Patent Quarterly dealing with the case of Stevens against the National Broadcasting Company, which was decided by the California Superior Court in 1966.

t. A book without place of publication, publisher, date of publication, or pagination. When a book lacks printed publication information or pagination, indicate this by using one or more of the following abbreviations:

n.p.   no place of publication given

n.p.   no publisher given

n.d.   no date of publication given

n. pag.   no pagination given (but see also Sec. 32v)

The abbreviation "n.p." should be placed *before* the colon to indicate "no place" but *after* the colon to indicate "no publisher."

No date: (New York: Univ. of Gotham Press, n.d.),

  p. 1.

No pagination: (New York: Univ. of Gotham Press,

  1978), n. pag.

No place: (n.p.: Univ. of Gotham Press, 1978),

  p. 1.

No publisher: (New York: n.p., 1978), p. 1.

Neither place nor publisher: (n.p.: n.p., 1978), p. 1.

If unstated information is known or ascertained, indicate it in brackets: (New York: Univ. of Gotham Press, [1978]). If little or no information can be ascertained, record what you know:

  64 Photographic View Album of Cambridge

([England]: n.p., n.d.), n. pag.

(Note that in the absence of a city of publication, stating the country is preferable to "n.p." for "no place.")

u. A book with multiple publishers. If two or more publishers are responsible for the publication of the book—not just two or more offices of the same publisher (see Sec. 31h)—then each should be indicated.

      [65] Wilmarth H. Starr, Mary P. Thompson, and Donald D. Walsh, eds., <u>Modern Foreign Languages and the Academically Talented Student</u> (Washington, D.C.: National Education Association; New York: MLA, 1960), p. 88.

Increasingly, British, Canadian, and American publishers co-operate in the publication of the same work; but this fact is often not stated in any edition of the work. For example, S. B. Harkness, *The Career of Samuel Butler, 1835-1902: A Bibliography* was published by both Macmillan in New York and Bodley Head Press in London, a fact that would not usually be known to a person consulting either one of the editions. In circumstances like this, cite the publishing information of the edition that you are using. If, however, you are preparing a list or bibliography and wish to indicate both publishers, follow the form of sample note 65 (and its related bibliographical form, Sec. 42u).

v. A book without page numbers but with signatures. Some books that lack page numbers, especially ones published before 1800, may include at the foot of every fourth page, every eighth page, every sixteenth page, and so on, a sequence of letters, numerals, or other symbols called signatures, which were intended to help the bookbinder assemble the groups of pages into the proper order. The pages following each new signature may bear the same symbol with an added numeral (either Arabic or Roman). In citing books without page numbers but with signatures, use the abbreviation "sig." or "sigs." (instead of "p." or "pp."), followed by the signature symbol and the leaf number (in Arabic). If no number is printed, supply one: the leaf on which a given signature first appears should be considered "1," the next leaf, "2," and so forth, until you reach a new signature. The front of a leaf—that appearing on the reader's right—is considered the "recto" (indicated as ^{r}); the back of the leaf—that appearing on the reader's left—is considered the "verso" (indicated as ^{v}).

66 John Pikeryng, <u>A Newe Enterlude of Vice</u>

<u>Conteyninge the Historye of Horestes</u> (London,

1567), sig. A2^r.

33 FIRST NOTE REFERENCES FOR ARTICLES IN PERIODICALS: STANDARD FORM

For examples of the various recommendations given in this section, see Sec. 34. In notes, the following order, subject to abridgment by omission of unnecessary items (see Sec. 32b), should be used (see Sec. 41 for the form of a listing in a bibliography).

a. Name(s) of author(s) in normal order, followed by a comma. Give the name(s) of the author(s) as printed on the first page or last page of the article. If only initials are given, indicate them all, and, in typing, leave a space after each period. If there is more than one author, treat as described for multiple authors of a book (see Sec. 32c).

b. Title of the article in full, enclosed in quotation marks (not underlined), followed by a comma inside the closing quotation marks unless the title has its own punctuation (e.g., a question mark).

c. Name of the periodical, underlined and followed by a comma. Common words within the name of a periodical may be abbreviated in accordance with standard usage (see Sec. 46). In citing the names of newspapers, give the name underlined, as it appears in the masthead; if the city is not part of the name as it appears in the masthead, supply it in square brackets, not underlined, following the name: *Star-Ledger* [Newark, N.J.]. Add names of cities or of institutions (in square brackets) to differentiate a given periodical from others with the same title or to locate an unfamiliar journal.

d. Series number, only if the journal is published in more than one series: *The Library*, 5th ser., 15 (1960); *Oxford Slavonic Papers*, NS 1 (1968), 85-104. The abbreviations "NS" and "OS" stand for "new series" and "original series," respectively, and are followed by the volume number in that series.

e. Volume number (not preceded by "Vol."), designated by an Arabic numeral, followed by a comma unless the next detail is enclosed in parentheses. For journals that have continuous pagination throughout the volume (i.e., if the last page of the first issue is numbered 130, then the first page of the second issue would be numbered 131, etc.), use the volume number followed by the year (in parentheses), a comma, and the page number(s): *Studies in Short Fiction*, 12 (1975), 91.

If, however, each issue of a volume is paged independently (i.e., each begins with p. 1), then specify in parentheses the month or season of the issue along with the year: (March 1975) or (Winter 1977); if the month or season is not known, indicate the issue number preceded by "No." following the volume number and comma and preceding the year in parentheses: *American-German Review,* 20, No. 5 (1954), 46. State issue number alone for journals that do not have volume numbers: *Fiera Letteraria*, No. 41 (1965), p. 6. For journals with a complex and unfamiliar numbering system, give all particulars known, citing the largest division first: Año 13, Tomo 41, No. 2.

Omit volume numbers and issue numbers of newspapers and weekly or monthly magazines and give the complete date instead, set off by commas and followed by the page numbers: *Chronicle of Higher Education*, 17 Jan. 1977, p. 5. Because different editions of newspapers contain different material, it is often useful to specify the edition: *New York Times*, Late City Ed., 29 Dec. 1968, p. 36, col. 1. With some newspapers, not even all copies labeled "Late City Ed." (or another edition) are necessarily identical; in such cases, the writer may have to ascertain the precise system of stars or other symbols that identifies a newspaper's disparate editions.

f. The year—preceded by month or season (e.g., Nov. or Autumn) only if pagination of each issue is separate—enclosed in parentheses (except for daily, weekly, or monthly publications), followed by a comma: *Renaissance Quarterly,* 29 (1976), 433; *Kansas Quarterly,* 3 (Spring 1971), 3-9. If the volume covers several years, list only the year of the article in question.

g. Page number(s) in Arabic numerals (preceded by "p." or "pp." only when no volume number is cited). Follow the page number with a period unless an additional reference to a note is needed (217n. or 217, n. 18.). For newspapers, it may be necessary to give section numbers, and it is convenient to include column numbers: *New York Times*, 21 Sept. 1969, Sec. 4, p. 14, cols. 4-6.

34 FIRST NOTE REFERENCES FOR ARTICLES IN PERIODICALS: SAMPLE NOTES

a. General remarks. Following are examples of the various recommendations in Sec. 33. For bibliographical examples that parallel the sample notes in each of these lettered subsections, see the corresponding lettered subsection of Sec. 43.

b. An article in a journal with continuous pagination throughout the annual volume. This is the basic form of reference to an article in a periodical.

67 Jarold W. Ramsey, "The Wife Who Goes Out

like a Man, Comes Back as a Hero: The Art of Two

Oregon Indian Narratives," <u>PMLA</u>, 92 (1977), 15.

For subsequent references to such articles, see Sec. 37.

c. An article from a journal that pages each issue separately or that numbers only issues.

68 John R. Frey, "America and Her Literature

Reviewed by Postwar Germany," <u>American-German</u>

<u>Review</u>, 20, No. 5 (1954), 4-6.

69 Donald Stephens and George Woodcock, "<u>The</u>

<u>Literary History of Canada</u>: Editorial Views,"

<u>Canadian Literature</u>, No. 24 (1965), p. 10.

70 Germain Marc'hadour, "Hugh Latimer and

Thomas More," <u>Moreana</u>, No. 18 (1968), pp. 29-49.

When no volume number is given, pages are identified by "p." or "pp."; issue numbers are given as Arabic numerals, preceded by "No." Months may be added for the sake of precision when the numbering system is unfamiliar.

d. An article from a journal with more than one series.

71 Yu. D. Levin, "Tolstoy, Shakespeare, and

Russian Writers of the 1860s," <u>Oxford Slavonic</u>

<u>Papers</u>, NS 1 (1968), 85-104.

e. An article from a weekly magazine or weekly newspaper.

72 Hennig Cohen, "Why Isn't Melville for the

Masses?" <u>Saturday Review</u>, 16 Aug. 1969, pp. 19-21.

[73] "The Old Art Forms Will Wither Away,"
<u>National Observer</u>, 22 Sept. 1969, p. 1, cols. 2-4;
p. 22, cols. 1-3.

f. An article from a monthly magazine.

[74] Irving Howe, "James Baldwin: At Ease in
Apocalypse," <u>Harper's</u>, Sept. 1968, p. 92.

g. An article from a daily newspaper. (For weekly newspapers, see Sec. 34e.)

[75] Jane E. Brody, "Multiple Cancers Termed on
Increase," <u>New York Times</u>, Late City Ed., 10 Oct.
1976, Sec. 1, p. 37, col. 1.

h. An editorial.

[76] "The Spirit of '77," Editorial, <u>Washington
Post</u>, 21 Jan. 1977, Sec. A, p. 22, cols. 1-2.

i. An anonymous article.

[77] "A Return to Guido Gozzano: An Italian
Poet Rediscovered," <u>Italy: Documents and Notes</u>, 17,
No. 1 (1968), 55-60.

j. A letter to the editor.

[78] Harry T. Moore, Letter, <u>Sewanee Review</u>, 71
(1963), 347-48.

k. Reviews, signed and unsigned. After the reviewer's name, state the title of the review (if there is one), the title and author of the work under review (preceded by "rev. of"), and the appropriate publication information. If the review is unsigned, begin the citation with the title of the review or, if untitled, simply with "Rev. of."

79 Melvin Maddocks, "Sermonets and Stoicism," rev. of <u>Not So Wild a Dream</u>, by Eric Sevareid, <u>Time</u>, 30 Aug. 1976, p. 69.

80 Patricia Merivale, rev. of <u>George Eliot and Flaubert: Pioneers of the Modern Novel</u>, by Barbara Smalley, <u>Comparative Literature Studies</u>, 13 (1976), 76-77.

81 "The Cooling of an Admiration," rev. of <u>Pound/Joyce: The Letters of Ezra Pound to James Joyce</u>, ed. Forrest Read, <u>Times Literary Supplement</u>, 6 March 1969, pp. 239-40.

82 Rev. of <u>Anthology of Danish Literature</u>, ed. F. J. Billeskov Jansen and P. M. Mitchell, <u>Times Literary Supplement</u>, 7 July 1972, p. 785.

l. An article whose title contains a quotation or a title within quotation marks.

83 Warren Carrier, "Commonplace Costumes and Essential Gaudiness: Wallace Stevens' 'The Emperor of Ice-Cream,'" <u>College Literature</u>, 1 (1974), 230.

On titles within titles, see Sec. 13c.

m. An article from *Dissertation Abstracts* or *Dissertation Abstracts International*. Beginning with Vol. 30 (1969), *Dissertation Abstracts (DA)* became *Dissertation Abstracts International (DAI)*. From Vol. 27 on, the *DA* and *DAI* are paginated in two series: "A" for humanities and social sciences, "B" for the sciences. It is useful to identify the degree-granting institution in parentheses at the end of a *DA* or *DAI* citation.

[84] Eric L. Gans, "The Discovery of Illusion: Flaubert's Early Works, 1835-1837," DA, 27 (1967), 3046A (Johns Hopkins).

35 FIRST NOTE REFERENCES FOR OTHER SOURCES

For bibliographical examples that parallel the sample notes in each of these lettered subsections, see the corresponding lettered subsection of Sec. 44.

a. Manuscripts and typescripts. In citing such sources, state, among other details, the location of the material, the identifying number (if any) that may have been assigned to it, and whether it is a manuscript (MS) or typescript (TS). Manuscripts are usually foliated (i.e., numbered by leaves rather than pages); use "fol." to indicate the leaf of a manuscript being quoted.

[85] Notebook 32, TS, p. 50. This and all other notebooks cited are in the Mark Twain Papers, Univ. of California, Berkeley.

[86] This is translated from the colophon of Bodley MS. 901.

[87] Bibliothèque Nationale MS. Nouv. Acq. 1159.

[88] Morgan Library MS. 819, fol. 17.

Note that in the above citations the location of the typescript from the Mark Twain Papers is explicitly stated but that the locations of the other manuscripts—the Bodleian and Morgan libraries and the Bibliothèque Nationale—are identified by being incorporated into the manuscript numbers.

b. Lectures. Give the speaker's name, the title of the lecture (if known) in quotation marks, the sponsoring organization (if applicable), the location, and the date.

[89] Madeleine Doran, "The Style and the Story: Shakespeare's Appropriate and Varying Artistry," English Section I, MLA Convention, San Francisco, 27 Dec. 1975.

c. Films. The citation must include the title (underlined), distributor, and date. Other information (writer, director, performers, producer, etc.) may be given if pertinent. Physical characteristics (e.g., size and length of film) may also be given (in parentheses after the date) if this information might be useful to the reader.

[90] Bernardo Bertolucci, dir., Last Tango in Paris, with Marlon Brando and Maria Schneider, United Artists, 1972.

d. Theatrical performances. References to theatrical performances should contain information similar to that given for films but should also include theater, city, and date of performance. In some cases, it is desirable to cite the conductor (cond.) or choreographer (chor.). The person cited first may vary, depending on the desired emphasis (cf. Secs. 32l and 32m).

[91] John Gielgud, dir., <u>Hamlet</u>, by Shakespeare, with Richard Burton, Shubert Theatre, Boston, 4 March 1964.

[92] John Kander and Fred Ebb, <u>Chicago</u>, dir. Bob Fosse, with Gwen Verdon, Chita Rivera, and Jerry Orbach, Forty-Sixth Street Theatre, New York, 20 Oct. 1975.

[93] Robert Shaw, cond., Atlanta Symphony Orchestra Concert, Atlanta Arts Center, 14 May 1974.

[94] Sarah Caldwell, dir. and cond., <u>La Traviata</u>, with Beverly Sills, Opera Company of Boston, Orpheum Theatre, Boston, 4 Nov. 1972.

[95] George Balanchine, chor., <u>Harlequinade</u>, New York City Ballet, New York State Theater, New York, 8 July 1968.

e. Musical compositions should be cited in the text if possible. If they must be cited in the notes—in order not to clutter the text with opus numbers, for example—follow the guidelines on titles in Sec. 13.

[96] Beethoven, Symphony No. 7 in A, op. 92.

f. Works of art should be cited in the text if possible. If a statue or painting must be cited in the notes, follow the guidelines on titles in Sec. 13. Remember to identify the institution housing the work (e.g., the museum) as well as the city. If only a photograph of the work is used, indicate this and include its source in citing the work.

⁹⁷ Rembrandt, <u>Aristotle Contemplating the Bust of Homer</u>, Metropolitan Museum of Art, New York.

⁹⁸ Jean-Antoine Houdon, <u>Statue of Voltaire</u>, Comédie Française, Paris; Illus. 51 in <u>Literature through Art: A New Approach to French Literature</u>, by Helmut A. Hatzfeld (New York: Oxford Univ. Press, 1952), p. 118.

g. Radio or television programs are cited as follows: title of program (underlined), network or local station and its city, and date of broadcast. Where appropriate, the title of the episode (in quotation marks) is given before the title of the program, and the title of the series (not underlined and not in quotation marks) is given after the program. Other information (director, narrator, producer) may be given if pertinent.

⁹⁹ "The Joy Ride," writ. Alfred Shaughnessy, <u>Upstairs, Downstairs</u>, created by Eileen Atkins and Jean Marsh, dir. Bill Bain, prod. John Hawkesworth, Masterpiece Theatre, introd. Alistair Cooke, PBS, 6 Feb. 1977.

¹⁰⁰ <u>The First Americans</u>, narr. Hugh Downs, writ. and prod. Craig Fisher, NBC News Special, 21 March 1968.

¹⁰¹ <u>The Black Cat</u>, dir. Hi Brown, CBS Mystery Theater, 4 Nov. 1973.

h. Recordings that are commercially available require a citation that includes composer (or performer), title of record or tape (or of the works on the recording), artist(s), manufacturer, catalog number, and year of issue (if unknown, indicate "n.d."; see Sec. 32t). The physical characteristics may be included (in parentheses) following the catalog number if the information is relevant or if the recording is not readily available (see sample note 107).

102 Giuseppe Verdi, <u>Rigoletto</u>, with Joan Sutherland, Luciano Pavarotti, Sherrill Milnes, and Martti Talvela, cond. Richard Bonynge, London Symphony Orchestra and Ambrosian Opera Chorus, London Records, OSA-12105, 1973.

103 Billie Holiday, "God Bless the Child," <u>Essential Billie Holiday</u>, Verve, 68410, 1961.

The title of a recording of classical music (e.g., *Mozart on a Summer's Evening*) is often less important than the list of works recorded and may be omitted from the citation. Titles of musical compositions, as mentioned above (Sec. 13a), are not underlined or put in quotation marks if identified only by form, number, and key.

104 Wolfgang A. Mozart, Divertimento in D (K. 334) and Notturno (Serenade) in D (K. 286), cond. Neville Mariner, Academy of St. Martin-in-the-Fields Orchestra, Argo, ZRG 705, 1973.

Recordings of the spoken word should be treated in the same way, usually with the speaker cited first.

105 Edward R. Murrow, <u>Year of Decision: 1943</u>, Columbia, CPS-3872, 1957.

35

Documentation

[106] Robert Frost, "Stopping by Woods on a Snowy Evening," <u>Robert Frost Reads His Poetry</u>, Caedmon, XC 783, 1952.

The titles of private or archival recordings and tapes should not be underlined. The date recorded (if known) and the location and identifying number of the recording should also be included.

[107] D. K. Wilgus, Southern Folk Tales, recorded 23-25 March 1965, Univ. of California, Los Angeles Archives of Folklore, B.76.82 ($7\frac{1}{2}$ ips, 7" reel).

Jacket notes, librettos, and other material accompanying a recording may be cited as follows:

[108] David Lewiston, Jacket Notes, <u>The Balinese Gamelan: Music from the Morning of the World</u>, Nonesuch Explorer Series, H-2015, n.d.

[109] Colette, Libretto, <u>L'Enfant et les sortilèges</u>, by Maurice Ravel, with Suzanne Danco and Hugues Cuenod, cond. Ernest Ansermet, Orchestre de la Suisse Romande, Richmond-London, SR 33086, n.d., p. 8.

[110] William Weaver, "The Making of <u>Turandot</u>," in Libretto, <u>Turandot</u>, by Giacomo Puccini, with Birgit Nilsson and Franco Corelli, cond. Francesco Molinari-Pradelli, Rome Opera House Orchestra and Chorus, Angel, CL-3671, 1966, pp. 5-6.

i. Personal letters fall into three general categories for the researcher: published letters, letters in archives, and letters received by the researcher. Treat published letters as works in a collection (see Secs. 32g and 32h), adding date of letter and number, if one has been assigned by the editor. In citing unpublished letters, follow the basic guidelines for manuscripts and typescripts (Sec. 35a) and for private and archival recordings and tapes (Sec. 35h).

111 "To George Henry Lewes," 6 March 1848, Letter 452, <u>Letters and Private Papers of William Makepeace Thackeray</u>, ed. Gordon N. Ray (Cambridge: Harvard Univ. Press, 1946), II, 353-54.

112 Thomas Hart Benton, Letter to John Charles Fremont, 22 June 1847, John Charles Fremont Papers, Southwest Museum Library, Los Angeles, Calif.

Cite a letter personally received as follows:

113 Letter received from Alexander Solzhenitsyn, 17 May 1976.

Some scholars use the abbreviations ALS (autograph letter signed) and TLS (typed letter signed) to distinguish between handwritten and typewritten letters.

j. Personal and telephone interviews require the name of the person making the statement and the date it was made. The note should specify at the outset the mode of communication.

114 Personal interview with Kurt Vonnegut, 27 July 1976.

[115] Telephone interview with Alvin F.

Poussaint, Professor of Psychiatry, Harvard

Medical School, 7 May 1975.

k. Documents from an information service. Treat documents secured from an information service—such as ERIC (Educational Resources Information Center) or NTIS (National Technical Information Service)—like other printed materials, adding a reference to the source. If the document was published separately from the information service, give full details of its original publication, followed by its identifying number in the information service.

[116] Bernard Spolsky, <u>Navajo Language</u>

<u>Maintenance: Six-Year-Olds in 1969</u>, Navajo Reading

Study Prog. Report No. 5 (Albuquerque: Univ. of

New Mexico, 1969), p. 22 (ERIC ED 043 004).

If the document was not previously published, treat the distribution of the document by the information service as the mode of publication.

[117] Paul R. Streiff, <u>Some Criteria for</u>

<u>Designing Evaluation of TESOL Programs</u> (ERIC ED 040

385), p. 10.

Note that there is no place of publication for documents distributed by EDRS (ERIC Document Reproduction Service), since the location of this government-sponsored service changes.

l. Indirect sources. Whenever possible, information should be taken from the original source, not a secondhand one. In some instances, however, the most direct source is an indirect one; for example, a spoken remark may be recorded in the journals of someone present when it was made or of someone to whom the remark was later retold.

118 Samuel Johnson, 20 March 1776, as quoted in James Boswell, <u>The Life of Johnson</u>, ed. George Birkbeck Hill and L. F. Powell, II (Oxford: Clarendon, 1934), 450.

On some occasions, it may be necessary to quote from a quotation within another book when the original book is not available. In these instances, give all information that is available to you about the original work.

119 Bernardo Segni, <u>Rettorica et poetica d'Aristotile</u> (Florence: L. Torrentino, 1549), p. 281, as quoted in Bernard Weinberg, <u>A History of Literary Criticism in the Italian Renaissance</u> (Chicago: Univ. of Chicago Press, 1961), I, 405.

120 Lionardo Salviati, <u>Poetica d'Aristotile parafrasata e comentata</u> (Florence, 1586), MS. II. II. 11., Bibl. Naz. Centrale, Florence, fol. 140^V, as quoted in Weinberg, I, 616-17.

36 CONSOLIDATION OF REFERENCES

Whenever feasible, consolidate references in your notes. The sources of several items within a sentence or paragraph can often be incorporated in the same note, with individual citations separated by semicolons.

121 This paper on how to prepare an index is

indebted to Kenneth L. Pike, "How to Make an
Index," <u>PMLA</u>, 83 (1968), 991-93; Robert L.
Collison, <u>Indexing Books</u> (New York: DeGraff, 1962);
Sina Spiker, <u>Indexing Your Book</u> (Madison: Univ. of
Wisconsin Press, 1964); and <u>A Manual of Style</u>,
12th ed. (Chicago: Univ. of Chicago Press, 1969),
pp. 399-430.

37 SUBSEQUENT REFERENCES TO A BOOK OR PERIODICAL

a. General remarks. After a work has been fully identified in a note, it is subsequently cited in shortened form. Be brief. Be clear. Make sure that the reader can recognize what work is being cited. In most cases, the author's last name alone, followed by relevant page numbers, will do. For example, a second or later reference to Northrop Frye's *Anatomy of Criticism,* cited above as sample note 1 (Sec. 32b), would simply be:

122 Frye, pp. 345-47.

The once popular abbreviations "op. cit." ("in the work cited") and "loc. cit." ("in the place cited") are now considered superfluous. If two or more authors with the identical surname or two or more works by the same author are cited—Frye's *Anatomy of Criticism* as well as his *The Critical Path*—citations after the first full reference note should include a shortened form of the title after the author's last name.

123 Frye, <u>Anatomy</u>, p. 278.

124 Frye, <u>Critical Path</u>, pp. 1-10.

If an unfamiliar abbreviation is used in repeated citations of a work, indicate in the first note the shortened form of subsequent references. Such short-form citations can and often should be included, within parentheses, in the body of the text instead of in the notes.

125 George Watson, ed., <u>The New Cambridge Bibliography of English Literature</u>, III (Cambridge: Cambridge Univ. Press, 1969), col. 270; hereafter cited as <u>NCBEL</u>.

For subsequent references to articles in periodicals, give the author's name and the page number(s). (In the absence of a volume number, remember to indicate "p." or "pp.") For example, a second or later reference to the article by Jarold W. Ramsey cited as sample note 67 (Sec. 34b) would be:

126 Ramsey, p. 16.

If two or more articles by the same author are being used, add a shortened form of the title: Ramsey, "The Wife Who Goes Out," p. 13.

Repeat information when two references in sequence refer to the same work; do not use "ibid." On frequent reference to the same work, see Secs. 13e and 37b.

b. Notes and parenthetical references combined. When dealing extensively with a single work (as in a term paper on a novel) or with several works by the same author, give in a note a first full reference to the edition being used and indicate all further references to that work parenthetically within the text.

Note:

127 Jonathan Swift, <u>Gulliver's Travels</u>, ed. Robert B. Heilman, rev. ed. (New York: Modern Library-Random House, 1969), Pt. I, Ch. iii

(p. 49). All further references to this work appear in the text.

Subsequent reference in text:

     In Brobdingnag, Gulliver is attacked by rats and by "above twenty wasps . . . humming louder than the drones of as many bagpipes" (Pt. II, Ch. iii; p. 123).

When the quotation is incorporated into the text, place the final period after the closing parenthesis, not before the closing quotation mark. When the quotation is set off from the text, place the period at the end of the quotation before the parenthetical statement and omit punctuation after the closing parenthesis.

Gulliver thus describes his encounter with the giant wasps of Brobdingnag:

         I remember one morning when . . . , after I had lifted up one of my sashes and sat down at my table to eat a piece of sweet cake for my breakfast, above twenty wasps, allured by the smell, came flying into the room, humming louder than the drones of as many bagpipes. Some of them seized my cake and carried it piecemeal away; others flew about my head and face, confounding me with the noise and putting me in the utmost

```
terror of their stings.  (Pt. II,

Ch. iii; p. 123)
```

It is usual—after specifying in a note the edition being used —to cite a play or long poem by a short title or familiar abbreviation and by main division and line numbers separated by periods (not commas) without spacing. Such a reference can usually be inserted within parentheses in the text immediately after the quotation. The most widely used and accepted abbreviations for the parts of the Bible and for Shakespeare's plays are listed in Sec. 49. Other abbreviations are also widely used (*FQ* for Spenser's *Faerie Queene, PL* for Milton's *Paradise Lost,* etc.). When in doubt about an abbreviation, consult the instructor or thesis adviser. An unfamiliar abbreviation should be explained, as in sample note 125 in Sec. 37a.

```
Iliad XI.19

1 Chron. xxi.8

Luke xiv.5

Oth. IV.ii.7-13

FQ III.iii.53.3
```

Notice that commas are not used after the titles in these references. If the title has been mentioned in the text or is clearly implied, it need not be repeated in the documentation. A growing tendency is to use Arabic numbers throughout (Luke 14.5, *FQ* 3.3.53.3); check your instructor's preference.

38 OTHER USES OF NOTES

Besides documenting assertions and quotations, notes may direct the reader's attention to previous studies that support, or disagree with, the ideas being presented or modified in the study. Writers who work with foreign languages sometimes place in a note the English translation of a passage quoted; those who are addressing an audience unlikely to know the foreign language frequently offer the translation in the text and the original in the note. Some writers use notes for peripheral explications or comments, but essay-like notes divert the reader's attention from the primary text. In general, omit exposition that cannot be accommodated in the text.

39 OTHER METHODS OF DOCUMENTATION

Parenthetical documentation (i.e., in the text) for *all* references is employed only in papers requiring very few citations or in bibliographical studies. If adopting this practice, remember to place *in the text* all the information normally found in the notes. The method may vary.

```
In Principles of Tragedy (Coral Gables, Fla.:

Univ. of Miami Press, 1968), p. 57, Geoffrey

Brereton states that. . . .


Klaus Weissenberger--Formen der Elegie von Goethe

bis Celan (Bern: Francke, 1969), p. 118--argues

that. . . .


John A. Jones (Pope's Couplet Art [Athens: Ohio

Univ. Press, 1969], p. 105) analyzes. . . .


Mary Ann Caws (The Presence of René Char,

Princeton: Princeton Univ. Press, 1976, pp. 322-24)

concludes. . . .
```

In scientific and technical writing, endnotes and footnotes are commonly omitted; instead, an author-date, author-title, or number system refers the reader to an appended bibliography, even for the initial citation of a work. In the author-date and author-title systems, only the author's last name, a shortened title (if more than one work by that author is being used) or the date of publication, and the page number(s) need be given.

```
Only one study has even touched upon this question

(Smith, 10-15).
```

```
Only one study has even touched upon this question

(Smith, Principles, 10-15).
```

```
Only one study has even touched upon this question

(Smith, 1972, 10-15).
```

Scientific and technical writers using the number system assign numbers to the works in the bibliography and cite in parenthetical documentation only the number of the work (sometimes underlined) and the page number(s).

```
Only one study has even touched upon this question

(36, 10-15).
```

Every field has its preferred format or "style." Available style manuals include the following:

Biology	Council of Biology Editors, Committee on Form and Style. *CBE Style Manual*. 3rd ed. Washington, D.C.: American Inst. of Biological Sciences, 1972.
Chemistry	American Chemical Society. *Handbook for Authors of Papers in the Journals of the American Chemical Society*. Washington, D.C.: American Chemical Soc., 1967.
Engineering	Engineers Joint Council, Committee of Engineering Society Editors. *Recommended Practice for Style of References in Engineering Publications*. New York: Engineers Joint Council, 1966.
Geology	U.S. Geological Survey. *Suggestions to Authors of Reports of the United States Geological Survey*. 5th ed. Washington, D.C.: GPO, 1958.

Linguistics	Linguistic Society of America. *LSA Bulletin*, No. 71 (Dec. 1976), pp. 43-45.
Mathematics	American Mathematical Society. *Manual for Authors of Mathematical Papers*. 4th ed. Providence, R.I.: American Mathematical Soc., 1971.
Medicine	American Medical Association, Division of Scientific Publications. *Style Book and Editorial Manual*. 4th ed. Chicago: American Medical Assn., 1966.
Physics	American Institute of Physics, Publications Board. *Style Manual*. Rev. ed. New York: American Inst. of Physics, 1973.
Physiology	"Suggestions to Authors," *Journal of Physiology*, 182 (1966), 1-33.
Psychology	American Psychological Association. *Publication Manual of the American Psychological Association*. 2nd ed. Washington, D.C.: American Psychological Assn., 1974.

BIBLIOGRAPHY

40 CONTENT, PLACEMENT, AND ARRANGEMENT OF THE BIBLIOGRAPHY [1]

a. Content. The bibliography of a research paper usually lists all the works referred to in the text and notes. It is called Bibliography or Works Cited (use the latter if it includes films, recordings, or other nonprint sources). A bibliography that contains descriptive or evaluative comments on bibliographical entries is entitled Annotated Bibliography or Annotated List of Works Cited. The title Works Consulted indicates the inclusion of works not cited in the text and notes. Avoid padding: do not list works you have not used (unless you are compiling the list for its own value).

b. Placement. The bibliography comes at the end of the research paper—followed in a book or dissertation by the index. It should begin on a new page (often without a number), its title appearing two inches from the top of the page (on margins and pagination, see respectively Secs. 20 and 24). Skip three lines (i.e., double-space twice) and begin the first bibliographical entry flush with the left-hand margin. The bibliography of a term paper is double-spaced (for dissertations, see Appendix, Sec. E). If an entry runs to more than one line, indent the second and subsequent lines five spaces. As with endnotes, continue the list on as many pages as necessary. Skip two spaces after each full stop. Number items in the bibliography only if you are using parenthetical documentation and the number system described in Sec. 39. In that case, place an Arabic numeral, followed by a period and a single space, before each entry.

[1] These instructions apply to the bibliography of a research paper, which is different from an elaborate and technical bibliographical description; for a thorough analysis of the problems involved in the latter, see Fredson T. Bowers, *Principles of Bibliographical Description* (1949; rpt. New York: Russell, 1962).

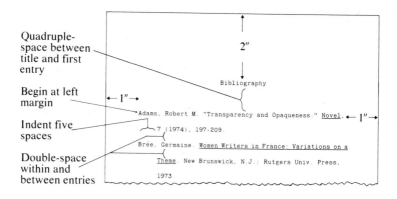

Quadruple-space between title and first entry

Begin at left margin

Indent five spaces

Double-space within and between entries

c. Arrangement. The bibliographical entries of a short paper are usually arranged in alphabetical order by the author's last name or, if anonymous, by title—determined by the first word other than a definite or indefinite article (*A Guide to Dining Out* is alphabetized under "G"). Occasionally, as in historical studies, the writer may wish to list items of the bibliography in chronological order, according to publication date; but this practice is rare.

If the bibliography is sizable, as in a dissertation, book, or long research paper, the writer may divide the bibliography into sections, with each section alphabetically arranged within itself. The bibliography may be divided simply into Primary Sources and Secondary Sources (see the sample pages at the conclusion of this handbook). In a paper dealing with several Renaissance poets, for instance, the works of the poets themselves would be listed under Primary Sources; the works of criticism, historical background, and similar material would be listed under Secondary Sources. Bibliographies are sometimes arranged according to research media: books, articles, recordings. Another method is to divide by subject matter. The list of works consulted for a study of several French statesmen, for example, might contain a separate section for each figure involved; the bibliography of a paper on Watergate could have such divisions as "Historical Background," "Legal Precedents," "Moral and Philosophical Issues," and "Political Consequences." A bibliographical arrangement could also be based on chronology or geography. The sections of a bibliography on capital punishment in the Western world could relate to periods of time: "Classical Greece and Rome," "The Middle Ages and Renaissance," and so forth; those on a study of famine in modern times, to places: "Asia," "Africa," and the like.

41 DIFFERENCES IN FORM BETWEEN NOTE AND BIBLIOGRAPHICAL CITATIONS

a. In general, the same information is contained in both the note and bibliographical citation. There are exceptions to this rule, however, as well as several differences in form.

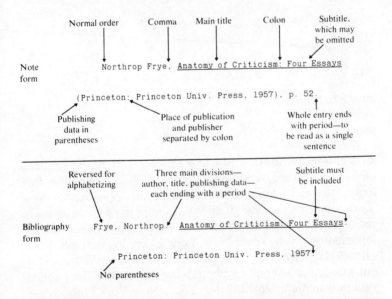

b. Name(s) of author(s) and title. In the bibliography, the author's name is reversed for alphabetizing. If there is more than one author, only the first name is reversed, followed by a comma: Wellek, René, and Austin Warren. The title in the bibliographical citation should be complete, including any subtitle; in the note, as stated above (Sec. 32b), it need not be complete. The treatment of titles (underlined or placed in quotation marks) is the same as in notes (see Sec. 13).

c. Publication information. As in a note, the place of publication and the publisher are separated by a colon, and the publisher and date by a comma; but this information is not enclosed in parentheses in the bibliography. In citations of periodicals, yearbooks, and reference books like the *DAB* and *DNB*, the year (sometimes preceded by the month or season) appears in parentheses following the volume number, edition, or title itself. The name of the degree-granting institution in the bibliographical citation of an article in *DA* or *DAI* also appears in parentheses.

Canadian Review of Comparative Literature, 2

  (1975), 201-27.

Who's Who in America. 37th ed. (1972-73).

DNB (1909).

DAI, 32 (1972), 3995A (Univ. of Southern

  California).

d. Volume numbers and page numbers. If all the volumes of a multivolume work have been used, indicate that fact *before* the publication information: 3 vols. New York: New York Univ. Press, 1968. If all the volumes have not been used, indicate the ones that have been used *after* the publication information: New York: New York Univ. Press, 1968. Vols. II and III. However, if the volumes were published in different years, the volume number(s) should precede the publication information: Vol. I. New York: New York Univ. Press, 1968. (For sample bibliographical entries for all three cases, see Sec. 42f.) Page numbers are seldom cited in the bibliography for books, but they are indicated for shorter pieces (articles, poems, short stories, essays) that appear within longer works (periodicals, anthologies, collections of essays). In such cases, give the page numbers of the *entire piece* (pp. 1-15), not just of the material directly used (p. 4). Page numbers follow a comma and are presented as part of the information that directly precedes them: New York: Macmillan, 1974, pp. 1-10.

e. Spacing and indentation. Whereas the first line of the note is indented five spaces and its second and subsequent lines begin at the left margin, the first line of the bibliographical entry extends to the left margin and its second and subsequent lines are indented five spaces.

f. Punctuation. In general, the bibliographical citation, unlike the note (see Sec. 27), is not to be read as if it were a sentence. Hence, complete blocks of information (including titles of articles in journals and periodicals) are followed by periods, not commas.

g. Two or more works by the same author(s) are indicated by giving the name(s) of the author(s) in the first entry only. Thereafter, in place of the name(s), type ten hyphens, follow with a period, skip two spaces, and give the next title. The ten hyphens stand for the full name in the preceding entry; if there is an additional author or authors, the name(s) of the additional author(s) may follow the hyphens. In citing two or more works by the same author(s) in the bibliography, the writer may arrange the titles either alphabetically or chronologically by date of publication.

Frye, Northrop. Anatomy of Criticism: Four Essays.

    Princeton: Princeton Univ. Press, 1957.

----------. The Critical Path: An Essay on the

    Social Context of Literary Criticism.

    Bloomington: Indiana Univ. Press, 1971.

----------, et al. Morality of Scholarship. Ed.

    Max Black. Studies in Humanities. Ithaca,

    N.Y.: Cornell Univ. Press, 1967.

42 SAMPLE BIBLIOGRAPHICAL ENTRIES FOR PUBLISHED BOOKS

a. In general, bibliographical entries for published books contain the same information normally contained in notes, but in the form and with the exceptions described in Sec. 41. For note citations that parallel the sample bibliographical entries in each of these lettered subsections, see the corresponding lettered subsection of Sec. 32.

b. A book with a single author. (Cf. Sec. 32b.)

Booth, Wayne C. <u>The Rhetoric of Fiction</u>. Chicago:

    Univ. of Chicago Press, 1961.

Frye, Northrop. <u>Anatomy of Criticism: Four Essays</u>.

    Princeton: Princeton Univ. Press, 1957.

Gelfand, Michael. <u>African Background: The</u>

    <u>Traditional Culture of the Shona-Speaking</u>

    <u>People</u>. Cape Town: Juta, 1965.

Meyer, Heinrich. <u>Goethe: Das Leben im Werk</u>.

    Stuttgart: Günther, 1967.

Sarin, Dharma P. <u>The Influence of Political</u>

    <u>Movements on Hindi Literature, 1906-1947</u>.

    Chandigarh: Punjab Univ. Publications Bureau,

    1968.

Note that the works cited in the sample notes in Sec. 32b have been alphabetized here as they normally would be for the bibliography. All subsequent examples of bibliographical entries follow the same practice.

c. A book with two or more authors. (Cf. Sec. 32c.)

Burn, Barbara B., et al. <u>Higher Education in Nine</u>
<u>Countries: A Comparative Study of Colleges and</u>
<u>Universities Abroad</u>. New York: McGraw-Hill,
1971.

Cargill, Oscar, William Charvat, and Donald D.
Walsh. <u>The Publication of Academic Writing</u>.
New York: MLA, 1966.

Wellek, René, and Austin Warren. <u>Theory of</u>
<u>Literature</u>. 3rd ed. New York: Harcourt,
1962.

d. A book with a corporate author. (Cf. Sec. 32d.)

<u>Higher Education for American Democracy</u>. By
the President's Commission on Higher
Education. Washington, D.C.: GPO, 1947.

or

President's Commission on Higher Education.
<u>Higher Education for American Democracy</u>.
Washington, D.C.: GPO, 1947.

<u>Report of the Commission on the Humanities</u>. New
York: American Council of Learned
Societies, 1964.

e. An anonymous book. (Cf. Sec. 32e.)

<u>Literary Market Place: The Directory of American
    Book Publishing</u>. 1976-77 ed. New York:
    Bowker, 1976.

<u>The World of Learning, 1975-76</u>. 26th ed. 2 vols.
    London: Europa, 1975.

f. A work in several volumes or parts. (Cf. Sec. 32f.)

Churchill, Winston S. <u>The Age of Revolution</u>. Vol.
    III of <u>A History of the English-Speaking
    Peoples</u>. New York: Dodd, Mead, 1957.

Daiches, David. <u>A Critical History of English
    Literature</u>. 2nd ed. New York: Ronald, 1970.
    Vol. II.

Parker, William R. <u>Milton: A Biography</u>. 2 vols.
    Oxford: Clarendon, 1968.

Wellek, René. <u>A History of Modern Criticism,
    1750-1950</u>. Vol. III. New Haven: Yale Univ.
    Press, 1965.

g. A work in a collection of pieces all by the same author. (Cf. Sec. 32g.)

Adam, Antoine. "Descartes." In <u>L'Epoque d'Henri
    IV et de Louis XIII</u>. Vol. I of <u>Histoire de la
    littérature française au XVIIe siècle</u>. Paris:
    Domat, 1948, pp. 319-29.

Malone, Kemp.   "Etymologies for <u>Hamlet</u>."   In his

    <u>Studies in Heroic Legend and in Current</u>

    <u>Speech</u>.   Ed. S. Einarsson and N. E. Eliason.

    Copenhagen: Rosenkilde and Bagger, 1959, pp.

    204-25.

h. A work in a collection of pieces by different authors.
(Cf. Sec. 32h.)

Hamilton, Marie Padgett.   "The Meaning of the

    Middle English <u>Pearl</u>."   <u>PMLA</u>, 70 (1955), 805-

    24.   Rpt. in <u>Middle English Survey: Critical</u>

    <u>Essays</u>.   Ed. Edward Vasta.   Notre Dame, Ind.:

    Univ. of Notre Dame Press, 1965, pp. 117-45.

Lewis, C. S.   "The Anthropological Approach."   In

    <u>English and Medieval Studies Presented to</u>

    <u>J. R. R. Tolkien on the Occasion of His</u>

    <u>Seventieth Birthday</u>.   Ed. Norman Davis and

    C. L. Wrenn.   London: Allen and Unwin, 1962,

    pp. 219-23.   Rpt. "View Points: C. S. Lewis."

    In <u>Twentieth Century Interpretations of</u> Sir

    Gawain and the Green Knight.   Ed. Denton Fox.

    Englewood Cliffs, N.J.: Prentice-Hall, 1968,

    pp. 100-01.

O'Connor, Flannery.   "Everything That Rises Must

    Converge."   In <u>Mirrors: An Introduction to</u>

    <u>Literature</u>.   Ed. John R. Knott, Jr., and

Christopher R. Reaske. 2nd ed. San

Francisco: Canfield, 1975, pp. 58-67.

Unamuno y Jugo, Miguel de. <u>Abel Sanchez</u>. Trans.

Anthony Kerrigan. In <u>Eleven Modern Short</u>

<u>Novels</u>. Ed. Leo Hamalian and Edmond L. Volpe.

2nd ed. New York: Putnam, 1970, pp. 253-344.

Wright, Richard. "Bright and Morning Star." In

<u>Short Stories: A Critical Anthology</u>. Ed.

Ensaf Thune and Ruth Prigozy. New York:

Macmillan, 1973, pp. 368-94.

If several works in the same collection have been cited in notes, the collection may be cited as a whole in the bibliography.

Thune, Ensaf, and Ruth Prigozy, eds. <u>Short</u>

<u>Stories: A Critical Anthology</u>. New York:

Macmillan, 1973.

Vasta, Edward, ed. <u>Middle English Survey: Critical</u>

<u>Essays</u>. Notre Dame, Ind.: Univ. of Notre

Dame Press, 1965.

i. Articles in reference works. (Cf. Sec. 32i.)

Chiappini, Luciano. "Este, House of."

<u>Encyclopaedia Britannica: Macropaedia</u>.

1974 ed.

French, John C. "Norris, Benjamin Franklin." <u>DAB</u>

(1934).

"Mandarin." <u>Encyclopedia Americana</u>. 1976 ed.

"Mead, Margaret." <u>Who's Who of American Women</u>.
8th ed. (1974-75).

Monkhouse, William Cosmo. "Reynolds, Sir Joshua."
<u>DNB</u> (1896).

j. A work in a series. (Cf. Sec. 32j.)

Fisher, John H. "The Progress of Research in
Medieval English Literature in the United
States of America." <u>English Studies Today</u>.
4th ser. Ed. Ilva Cellini and Giorgio
Melchiori. Rome: Edizioni di Storia e
Letteratura, 1966, pp. 33-43.

Hoefert, Sigfrid. <u>Das Drama des Naturalismus</u>.
Sammlung Metzler, 75. Stuttgart: Metzler,
1968.

Wallerstein, Ruth C. <u>Richard Crashaw: A Study in
Style and Poetic Development</u>. Univ. of
Wisconsin Studies in Lang. and Lit., No. 37.
Madison: Univ. of Wisconsin Press, 1935.

k. A modern reprint of an older edition. (Cf. Sec. 32k.)

Bray, René. <u>La Formation de la doctrine classique
en France</u>. 1927; rpt. Paris: Nizet, 1966.

Lowes, John Livingston. <u>The Road to Xanadu: A</u>

<u>Study in the Ways of the Imagination</u>. 2nd ed.

1930; rpt. New York: Vintage-Knopf, 1959.

Willey, Basil. <u>The Eighteenth Century Background:</u>

<u>Studies on the Idea of Nature in the Thought</u>

<u>of the Period</u>. London, 1940; rpt. Boston:

Beacon, 1961.

l. An edition. (Cf. Sec. 321.)

Cook, Don L., gen. ed. <u>A Selected Edition of</u>

<u>W. D. Howells</u>. Vol. XVI: <u>A Hazard of New</u>

<u>Fortunes</u>. Ed. David J. Nordloh et al.

Bloomington: Indiana Univ. Press, 1976.

Hinman, Charlton, ed. <u>The First Folio of</u>

<u>Shakespeare: The Norton Facsimile</u>. New York:

Norton, 1968.

Smith, Henry Nash, introd. <u>The Prairie: A Tale</u>.

By James Fenimore Cooper. New York: Holt,

1950.

or

Cooper, James Fenimore. <u>The Prairie: A Tale</u>.

Introd. Henry Nash Smith. New York: Holt,

1950.

m. A translation. (Cf. Sec. 32m.)

Coulson, Jessie, trans. <u>Crime and Punishment</u>.

By Feodor Dostoevsky. Ed. George Gibian.

New York: Norton, 1964.

or

Dostoevsky, Feodor. <u>Crime and Punishment</u>.

Trans. Jessie Coulson. Ed. George Gibian.

New York: Norton, 1964.

Sastre, Alfonso. <u>Sad Are the Eyes of William</u>

<u>Tell</u>. Trans. Leonard C. Pronko. In <u>The</u>

<u>New Wave Spanish Drama</u>. Ed. George E.

Wellwarth. New York: New York Univ. Press,

1970, pp. 265-321.

Schoolfield, George C., trans. <u>The German Lyric</u>

<u>of the Baroque in English Translation</u>. Univ.

of North Carolina Studies in Germanic

Langs. and Lits., 29. Chapel Hill: Univ.

of North Carolina Press, 1961.

n. An unpublished dissertation. (Cf. Sec. 32n.)

Gans, Eric L. "The Discovery of Illusion:

Flaubert's Early Works, 1835-1837." Diss.

Johns Hopkins 1967.

o. A published dissertation. (Cf. Sec. 32o.)

Nykrog, Per. <u>Les Fabliaux: Etude d'histoire</u>

<u>littéraire et de stylistique médiévale</u>. Diss.

Aarhus 1956. Copenhagen: Munksgaard, 1957.

Wendriner, Karl Georg. <u>Der Einfluss von Goethes</u>

Wilhelm Meister <u>auf das Drama der Romantiker</u>.
Diss. Bonn 1907. Leipzig: privately printed,
1907.

p. The published proceedings of a conference. (Cf. Sec. 32p.)

<u>Humanistic Scholarship in America</u>. Proc. of a
Conference on the Princeton Studies in the
Humanities. 5-6 Nov. 1965. Princeton:
Princeton Univ., 1966.

q. A pamphlet. (Cf. Sec. 32q.)

Modern Language Association of America. <u>A Guide
for Job Candidates and Department Chairmen in
English and Foreign Languages</u>. Rev. ed. New
York: MLA, 1975.

r. Government publications. (Cf. Sec. 32r.)

<u>Cong. Rec</u>. 7 Feb. 1973, pp. 3831-51.
Great Britain. Ministry of Defence. <u>Author and
Subject Catalogues of the Naval Library,
Ministry of Defence</u>. London: HMSO, 1967.
New York City. Knapp Commission. <u>The Knapp
Commission Report on Police Corruption</u>. New
York: Braziller, [1973?].
New York State. Committee on State Prisons.

Investigation of the New York State Prisons.

1883; rpt. New York: Arno, 1974.

United Nations. Economic Commission for Africa.

Industrial Growth in Africa. New York:

United Nations, 1963.

U.S. Bureau of Labor Statistics. Productivity.

Washington, D.C.: GPO, 1958.

U.S. Cong. Joint Committee on the Investigation

of the Pearl Harbor Attack. Hearings.

79th Cong., 1st and 2nd sess. 32 vols.

Washington, D.C.: GPO, 1946.

U.S. Cong. Senate. Special Committee to

Investigate Organized Crime in Interstate

Commerce. Report on Crime Investigation.

82nd Cong., 1st sess. S. Rept. 141.

Washington, D.C.: GPO, 1951.

Washburne, E. B. Memphis Riots and Massacres.

U.S. 39th Cong., 2nd sess. H. Rept. 101.

1866; rpt. New York: Arno, 1969.

or

U.S. Cong. House. Memphis Riots and Massacres.

By E. B. Washburne. 39th Cong., 2nd sess.

H. Rept. 101. 1866; rpt. New York: Arno,

1969.

s. Legal references. (Cf. Sec. 32s.)

Stevens v. National Broadcasting Co. 148 U.S.P.Q.

755. Cal. Super. Ct. 1966.

15 U.S. Code. Sec. 78j(b) (1964).

U.S. Const. Art. I, sec. 1.

t. A book without place of publication, publisher, date of publication, or pagination. (Cf. Sec. 32t.)

Photographic View Album of Cambridge. [England]:

n.p., n.d.

u. A book with multiple publishers. (Cf. Sec. 32u.)

Starr, Wilmarth H., Mary P. Thompson, and Donald D.

Walsh, eds. Modern Foreign Languages and the

Academically Talented Student. Washington,

D.C.: National Education Association; New

York: MLA, 1960.

v. A book without page numbers but with signatures. (Cf. Sec. 32v.)

Pikeryng, John. A Newe Enterlude of Vice

Conteyninge the Historye of Horestes. London,

1567.

43 SAMPLE BIBLIOGRAPHICAL ENTRIES FOR ARTICLES IN PERIODICALS

a. In general, bibliographical entries for articles in periodicals should contain the information normally contained in notes but in the form and with the exceptions described in Sec. 41. For notes that parallel the sample bibliographical entries in each of these lettered subsections, see the corresponding lettered subsection of Sec. 34.

b. An article in a journal with continuous pagination throughout the annual volume. (Cf. Sec. 34b.)

Ramsey, Jarold W. "The Wife Who Goes Out like a

Man, Comes Back as a Hero: The Art of Two

Oregon Indian Narratives." PMLA, 92 (1977),

9-18.

c. An article from a journal that pages each issue separately or that numbers only issues. (Cf. Sec. 34c.)

Frey, John R. "America and Her Literature

Reviewed by Postwar Germany." American-

German Review, 20, No. 5 (1954), 4-6.

Marc'hadour, Germain. "Hugh Latimer and Thomas

More." Moreana, No. 18 (1968), pp. 29-49.

Stephens, Donald, and George Woodcock. "The

Literary History of Canada: Editorial Views."

Canadian Literature, No. 24 (1965), pp. 10-22.

d. An article from a journal with more than one series. (Cf. Sec. 34d.)

Levin, Yu. D. "Tolstoy, Shakespeare, and Russian

Writers of the 1860s." Oxford Slavonic

Papers, NS 1 (1968), 85-104.

e. An article from a weekly magazine or weekly newspaper. (Cf. Sec. 34e.)

Cohen, Hennig. "Why Isn't Melville for the

  Masses?" Saturday Review, 16 Aug. 1969,

  pp. 19-21.

"The Old Art Forms Will Wither Away." National

  Observer, 22 Sept. 1969, p. 1, cols. 2-4; p.

  22, cols. 1-3.

f. An article from a monthly magazine. (Cf. Sec. 34f.)

Howe, Irving. "James Baldwin: At Ease in

  Apocalypse." Harper's, Sept. 1968, pp.

  92-100.

g. An article from a daily newspaper. (Cf. Sec. 34g.)

Brody, Jane E. "Multiple Cancers Termed on

  Increase." New York Times, Late City Ed., 10

  Oct. 1976, Sec. 1, p. 37, col. 1.

h. An editorial. (Cf. Sec. 34h.)

"The Spirit of '77." Editorial. Washington Post,

  21 Jan. 1977, Sec. A, p. 22, cols. 1-2.

i. An anonymous article. (Cf. Sec. 34i.)

"A Return to Guido Gozzano: An Italian Poet

  Rediscovered." Italy: Documents and Notes,

  17, No. 1 (1968), 55-60.

j. A letter to the editor. (Cf. Sec. 34j.)

Moore, Harry T. Letter. <u>Sewanee Review</u>, 71
(1963), 347-48.

k. Reviews, signed and unsigned. (Cf. Sec. 34k.)

Rev. of <u>Anthology of Danish Literature</u>, ed. F. J.
Billeskov Jansen and P. M. Mitchell. <u>Times
Literary Supplement</u>, 7 July 1972, p. 785.

"The Cooling of an Admiration." Rev. of
<u>Pound/Joyce: The Letters of Ezra Pound to
James Joyce</u>, ed. Forrest Read. <u>Times
Literary Supplement</u>, 6 March 1969, pp. 239-40.

Maddocks, Melvin. "Sermonets and Stoicism." Rev.
of <u>Not So Wild a Dream</u>, by Eric Sevareid.
<u>Time</u>, 30 Aug. 1976, p. 69.

Merivale, Patricia. Rev. of <u>George Eliot and
Flaubert: Pioneers of the Modern Novel</u>, by
Barbara Smalley. <u>Comparative Literature
Studies</u>, 13 (1976), 76-77.

l. An article whose title contains a quotation or a title within quotation marks. (Cf. Sec. 34l.)

Carrier, Warren. "Commonplace Costumes and
Essential Gaudiness: Wallace Stevens' 'The
Emperor of Ice-Cream.'" <u>College Literature</u>,
1 (1974), 230-35.

m. An article from *Dissertation Abstracts* or *Dissertation Abstracts International*. (Cf. Sec. 34m.)

Gans, Eric L.   "The Discovery of Illusion:

Flaubert's Early Works, 1835-1837."   <u>DA</u>, 27

(1967), 3046A (Johns Hopkins).

44 SAMPLE BIBLIOGRAPHICAL ENTRIES FOR OTHER SOURCES

For notes that parallel the sample bibliographical entries in each of these lettered subsections, see the corresponding lettered subsection of Sec. 35.

a. Manuscripts and typescripts. (Cf. Sec. 35a.)

Twain, Mark.   Notebook 32, TS.   Mark Twain Papers.

Univ. of California, Berkeley.

b. Lectures. (Cf. Sec. 35b.)

Doran, Madeleine.   "The Style and the Story:

Shakespeare's Appropriate and Varying

Artistry."   English Section I, MLA

Convention, San Francisco.   27 Dec. 1975.

c. Films. (Cf. Sec. 35c.)

Bertolucci, Bernardo, dir.   <u>Last Tango in Paris</u>.

With Marlon Brando and Maria Schneider.

United Artists, 1972.

d. Theatrical performances. (Cf. Sec. 35d.)

Balanchine, George, chor. <u>Harlequinade</u>. New York
    City Ballet. New York State Theater, New
    York. 8 July 1968.

Caldwell, Sarah, dir. and cond. <u>La Traviata</u>.
    With Beverly Sills. Opera Company of
    Boston. Orpheum Theatre, Boston. 4 Nov.
    1972.

Gielgud, John, dir. <u>Hamlet</u>. By Shakespeare.
    With Richard Burton. Shubert Theatre,
    Boston. 4 March 1964.

Kander, John, and Fred Ebb. <u>Chicago</u>. Dir. Bob
    Fosse. With Gwen Verdon, Chita Rivera, and
    Jerry Orbach. Forty-Sixth Street Theatre,
    New York. 20 Oct. 1975.

Shaw, Robert, cond. Atlanta Symphony Orchestra
    Concert. Atlanta Arts Center, Atlanta. 14
    May 1974.

e. Musical compositions. (Cf. Sec. 35e.)

Beethoven, Ludwig van. Symphony No. 7 in A, op.
    92.

f. Works of art. (Cf. Sec. 35f.)

Houdon, Jean-Antoine. <u>Statue of Voltaire</u>. Comédie

Française, Paris. Illus. 51 in <u>Literature</u>
<u>through Art: A New Approach to French</u>
<u>Literature</u>. By Helmut A. Hatzfeld. New
York: Oxford Univ. Press, 1952.

Rembrandt van Rijn. <u>Aristotle Contemplating the</u>
<u>Bust of Homer</u>. Metropolitan Museum of Art,
New York.

g. Radio or television programs. (Cf. Sec. 35g.)

<u>The Black Cat</u>. Dir. Hi Brown. CBS Mystery
Theater. 4 Nov. 1973.

<u>The First Americans</u>. Narr. Hugh Downs. Writ.
and prod. Craig Fisher. NBC News Special.
21 March 1968.

"The Joy Ride." Writ. Alfred Shaughnessy.
<u>Upstairs, Downstairs</u>. Created by Eileen
Atkins and Jean Marsh. Dir. Bill Bain.
Prod. John Hawkesworth. Masterpiece Theatre.
Introd. Alistair Cooke. PBS, 6 Feb. 1977.

h. Recordings. (Cf. Sec. 35h.)

Colette. Libretto. <u>L'Enfant et les sortilèges</u>.
By Maurice Ravel. With Suzanne Danco and
Hugues Cuenod. Cond. Ernest Ansermet,
Orchestre de la Suisse Romande. Richmond-
London, SR 33086, n.d.

Frost, Robert. Robert Frost Reads His Poetry.

    Caedmon, XC 783, 1952.

Holiday, Billie. Essential Billie Holiday. Verve,

    68410, 1961.

Lewiston, David. Jacket Notes. The Balinese

    Gamelan: Music from the Morning of the World.

    Nonesuch Explorer Series, H-2015, n.d.

Mozart, Wolfgang A. Divertimento in D (K. 334)

    and Notturno (Serenade) in D (K. 286). Cond.

    Neville Mariner, Academy of St. Martin-in-

    the-Fields Orchestra. Argo, ZRG 705, 1973.

Murrow, Edward R. Year of Decision: 1943.

    Columbia, CPS-3872, 1957.

Verdi, Giuseppe. Rigoletto. With Joan

    Sutherland, Luciano Pavarotti, Sherrill

    Milnes, and Martti Talvela. Cond. Richard

    Bonynge, London Symphony Orchestra and

    Ambrosian Opera Chorus. London Records,

    OSA-12105, 1973.

Weaver, William. "The Making of Turandot." In

    Libretto. Turandot. By Giacomo Puccini.

    With Birgit Nilsson and Franco Corelli.

    Cond. Francesco Molinari-Pradelli, Rome

    Opera House Orchestra and Chorus. Angel,

    CL-3671, 1966.

Wilgus, D. K. Southern Folk Tales. Recorded
23-25 March 1965. Univ. of California, Los
Angeles Archives of Folklore, B.76.82 (7½
ips, 7" reel).

i. Personal letters. (Cf. Sec. 35i.)

Benton, Thomas Hart. Letter to Charles Fremont.
22 June 1847. John Charles Fremont Papers.
Southwest Museum Library, Los Angeles, Calif.

Ray, Gordon N., ed. <u>Letters and Private Papers of
William Makepeace Thackeray</u>. 4 vols.
Cambridge: Harvard Univ. Press, 1946.

Solzhenitsyn, Alexander. Letter to author. 17
May 1976.

j. Personal and telephone interviews. (Cf. Sec. 35j.)

Poussaint, Alvin F. Telephone interview. 7 May
1975.

Vonnegut, Kurt. Personal interview. 27 July 1976.

k. Documents from an information service. (Cf. Sec. 35k.)

Spolsky, Bernard. <u>Navajo Language Maintenance:
Six-Year-Olds in 1969</u>. Navajo Reading Study
Prog. Report No. 5. Albuquerque: Univ. of
New Mexico, 1969. ERIC ED 043 004.

Streiff, Paul R. <u>Some Criteria for Designing</u>

Evaluation of TESOL Programs. ERIC

ED 040 385.

I. Indirect sources. (Cf. Sec. 351.)

Boswell, James. The Life of Johnson. Ed.

George Birkbeck Hill and L. F. Powell. 6

vols. Oxford: Clarendon, 1934-50.

Weinberg, Bernard. A History of Literary Criticism

in the Italian Renaissance. 2 vols. Chicago:

Univ. of Chicago Press, 1961.

ABBREVIATIONS AND REFERENCE WORDS

45 GENERAL REMARKS

Common sense should guide the use of abbreviations in notes
and bibliographies. Economy of space is important, but clarity
more so.

46 ABBREVIATIONS

In notes and bibliographies, use common abbreviations of
dates (Feb., 18th century), of *institutions* (Acad., Assn.,
Coll., Dept., Inst., Soc., Univ.), of *publications* (Bull., Diss.,
Jour., Mag.), and of *states and countries* (Fla. or FL, Eng.).
In linguistic studies where the context makes them clear, use
abbreviations before quoted forms: E or Eng., Fr., Ger., Gk.,
It., L or Lat., ME, MHG, OE, OF or OFr., OHG, OIr.,
Prov., Sp., and so forth. Abbreviations that end in a small letter
are followed by a period. A person's initials are always
spaced. Abbreviations with more than two letters and those
omitting periods are never spaced; practice with regard to
two-letter abbreviations with periods varies.

```
H. N. Smith              Ph.D.

M.A.                     L. C.

MLA                      Washington, D.C.
```

A tendency in documentation is to omit periods in abbreviations consisting of the initials of well-known periodicals (*TLS*
for *Times Literary Supplement*), learned societies and professional organizations (AMA, ACLS), and books (*DNB*, not
DNB., although *D.N.B.* or *Dict. Nat. Biog.* is equally correct; *OED*, formerly known as *N.E.D.*; *DAB*). It should be
noted that some journals—among others, *ELH* and *PMLA*—
have initial letter abbreviations (without periods) as actual titles and also that most journals with single-word titles (*Specu-*

lum) have no widely accepted abbreviations. Generally speaking, in citing periodicals, abbreviate only those titles likely to be familiar to the reader. Professional scholars in all disciplines tend to refer to journals and reference works within their discipline by acronyms: *CBEL* for *Cambridge Bibliography of English Literature*; *JEGP* for *Journal of English and Germanic Philology*. (A list of acronyms for journals in the field of modern languages and literatures appears in the front of each edition of the *MLA International Bibliography*.) Unless your intended audience is familiar with these acronyms, do not use them. Instead, abbreviate common words in order to save space.

47 USE OF ITALICS IN ABBREVIATIONS

As noted above (Sec. 10h), accepted style has long been to underline unquoted foreign words and phrases in an English text but not to underline such words when familiarity and continued use have added them to the English stock. This convention has been widely applied to many common abbreviations of Latin words (A.D., p.m., P.S., cf., e.g., etc., i.e., viz., vs.) and by most instructors and scholarly writers to some of the abbreviations used in scholarship (et seq., q.v., s.v.).

48 LIST OF COMMON ABBREVIATIONS AND REFERENCE WORDS

acad.	academy
A.D.	*anno Domini* 'in the year of the Lord.' No space between; precedes numerals (A.D. 14). Cf. "B.C."
ALS	autograph letter signed
anon.	anonymous
ante	'before.' But "before" is preferred.
app.	appendix
art., arts.	article(s)
assn.	association
b.	born (Lat., Fr., It., Sp. "n."; Ger. "geb.")
B.C.	before Christ. No space between; follows numerals (19 B.C.). Cf. "A.D."

B.C.E.	before Common Era. No spaces between.
bibliog.	bibliography, bibliographer, bibliographical
biog.	biography, biographer, biographical
bk., bks.	book(s)
B.M.	British Museum, London (now British Library). No space between.
B.N.	Bibliothèque Nationale. No space between.
bull.	bulletin
©	copyright (© 1977)
c., ca.	*circa* 'about.' Used with approximate dates (c. 1796).
C.E.	Common Era. No space between.
cf.	*confer* 'compare.' Never use "cf." when "see" is intended. (Ger. "vgl.")
ch., chs. (or chap., chaps.)	chapters(s)
chor., chors.	choreographed by, choreographer(s)
col., cols.	column(s)
coll.	college
comp., comps.	compiled by, compiler(s)
cond.	conducted by, conductor
Cong.	Congress
Cong. Rec.	*Congressional Record*
d.	died (Lat. "ob."; Ger. "gest."; Fr. and Sp. "m.")
DA, DAI	*Dissertation Abstracts, Dissertation Abstracts International*
D.A.	Doctor of Arts. No space between.
DAB	*Dictionary of American Biography*
dept.	department
dir., dirs.	directed by, director(s)
diss.	dissertation
DNB	*Dictionary of National Biography*
doc., docs.	document(s)
E, Eng.	English
ed., eds.	edited by, editor(s), edition(s). Some prefer "edn." for "edition."
ed. cit.	*editio citata* 'edition cited.' Avoid using.
e.g.	*exempli gratia* 'for example.' Rarely capital-

ized; no space between; set off by commas. (Ger. "z.B."; Fr. "p.ex."; It. "p.es."; Sp. "por ej.")

enl.	enlarged (as in "rev. and enl. ed.")
esp.	especially (as in "pp. 248-63, esp. p. 251")
et al. (never et als.)	*et alii* 'and others'
et seq.	*et sequens, sequentia* 'and the following.' But see "f., ff."
etc.	*et cetera* 'and so forth.' Avoid using in text. (Ger. "usw.")
ex., exs.	example(s)
f., ff.	and the following (with a space after a numeral) page(s) or line(s). But exact references are preferable: pp. 53-54 instead of pp. 53 f.; pp. 53-58 instead of pp. 53 ff.
facsim. (or facs.)	facsimile
fasc.	fascicle
fig., figs.	figure(s)
fl.	*floruit* 'flourished, reached greatest development or influence.' Used before dates of historical figures when birth and death dates are not known.
fn.	footnote. "n." is preferred.
fol., fols.	folio(s)
Fr.	French
front.	frontispiece
GPO	Government Printing Office, Washington, D.C.
Ger.	German
Gk.	Greek
H. Doc.	House Document
hist.	history, historian, historical
HMSO	Her (His) Majesty's Stationery Office
H.R.	House of Representatives. No space between.
H. Rept.	House Report
H. Res.	House Resolution
ibid. (sometimes ib.)	*ibidem* 'in the same place,' i.e., the single title cited in the note immediately preceding.

48 Abbreviations and Reference Words

	Not to be introduced by "in." May be followed by page number(s) preceded by "p." or "pp." Avoid using ibid. (Ger. "ebd.")
i.e.	*id est* 'that is.' Rarely capitalized; no space between; set off by commas. (Ger. "d.h.")
illus.	illustrated (by), illustrator, illustration(s)
infra	'below.' But "below" is preferred.
inst.	institute, institution
introd.	(author of) introduction, introduced by, introduction
ips	inches per second (used in reference to recording tapes)
It.	Italian
jour.	journal
l., ll.	line(s)
lang., langs.	language(s)
L, Lat.	Latin
L. C.	Library of Congress. Usually a space between.
loc. cit. (not l.c.)	*loco citato* 'in the place (passage) cited,' i.e., in the same passage referred to in a recent note. Never follow "loc. cit." with a page number. (Ger. "a.a.O.") Repeating the page is as easy for the writer and more convenient for the reader. Avoid using.
M.A.	Master of Arts. No space between.
mag.	magazine
ME	Middle English
MHG	Middle High German
ms, mss	manuscript(s) (the many mss of Chaucer). Capitalize MS and follow it with a period when referring to a specific manuscript (Bodleian MS. Tanner 43).
M.S.	Master of Science. No space between.
n., nn.	note(s) (p. 56, n. 3). Preferred to "fn."; occasionally written without a period and closed up to the page number: p. 56n. (Ger. "Anm.")
narr., narrs.	narrated by, narrator(s)
N.B.	*nota bene* 'take notice, mark well.' No space between.

n.d.	no date (in a book's imprint). No space between. (Ger. "o.J."; Fr. "s.d."; Sp. "s.f.")
N.E.D.	*New English Dictionary*. No spaces between. Cf. *OED*.
no., nos.	number(s). Cf. "numb."
n.p.	no place (of publication) (Ger. "o.O."; Fr. and Sp. "s.l."); no publisher. No space between.
n. pag.	no pagination. Space between.
NS (or N.S.)	New Series; New Style (calendar)
numb.	numbered
OE	Old English
OED	*Oxford English Dictionary*. Formerly the *New English Dictionary (N.E.D.)*
OF, OFr.	Old French
OHG	Old High German
OIr.	Old Irish
op.	opus (work)
op. cit.	*opere citato* 'in the work cited.' The most abused of scholarly abbreviations, it is properly used in citing a passage on a different page (cf. "loc. cit.") of a work recently noted, but in such instances the author's name alone may suffice or the name and a short title may be clearer. Avoid using.
OS (or O.S.)	Old Series, Original Series; Old Style (calendar)
p., pp.	page(s). Omit if volume number precedes. (Ger. "S."; Sp. "pág., págs.")
par., pars.	paragraph(s)
passim	'throughout the work, here and there' (as "pp. 78, 111, et passim")
Ph.D.	Doctor of Philosophy. No space between.
philol.	philological
philos.	philosophical
pl., pls.	plate(s)
post	'after.' But "after" is preferred.
pref.	preface ("by" understood in context)
proc.	proceedings
prod., prods.	produced by, producer(s)

Prov.	Provençal
pseud.	pseudonym
pt., pts.	part(s)
pub. (or publ.), pubs.	published by, publication(s)
q.v.	*quod vide* 'which see.' No space between.
r (super-scribed, no period)	*recto* 'righthand page' (as B4^r); or, when describing a single sheet, the front. See "v" and Sec. 32v.
reg.	registered
rept., repts.	reported by, report(s)
res.	resolution
resp.	respectively (pp. 56, 17, 89, 6, resp.)
rev.	revised (by), revision; review, reviewed (by). It is better to spell out "review" if there is any possibility of ambiguity.
rpm	revolutions per minute (used of recordings)
rpt.	reprinted (by), reprint
S.	Senate
sc.	scene (Sp. "esc.")
S. Doc.	Senate Document
sec., secs. (or sect., sects.)	section(s)
ser.	series
sess.	session
sic	'thus, so.' Between square brackets when used as an editorial interpolation (see Sec. 14e); otherwise within parentheses. Avoid using with an exclamation mark.
sig., sigs.	signature(s)
soc.	society
Sp.	Spanish
S. Rept.	Senate Report
S. Res.	Senate Resolution
st., sts.	stanza(s)
St., Sts. (or now rarely S., SS)	Saint(s) (Fr. fem. "Ste, Stes")
sup.	*supra* 'above.' But "above" is preferred.

supp., supps.	supplement(s)
s.v.	*sub verbo* or *voce* 'under the word or heading.' No space between.
TLS	typed letter signed
trans. (or tr.)	translated by, translator, translation
TS	typescript. Cf. "ms."
univ.	university
v (superscribed, no period)	*verso* 'left-hand page' (as B4ᵛ); or, when describing a single sheet, the back. See "r" and Sec. 32v.
v.	*vide* 'see' (Ger. "s.")
v., vs.	versus 'against.' Cf. "v., vv."
v., vv. (or vs., vss.)	verse(s). Cf. "v., vs."
v.d.	various dates. No space between. Avoid using.
viz.	*videlicet* 'namely.' With or without a period; usage varies. Avoid using.
vol., vols.	volume(s) (Vol. II of 3 vols.). Omit "Vol." and "p." when both items are supplied. (Ger. "Bd., Bde."; Sp. "t.")

49 ABBREVIATIONS FOR THE BIBLE AND WORKS OF SHAKESPEARE

The following abbreviations may be used in notes and parenthetical references; they should not be used in the text (except parenthetically).

a. Bible.

Old Testament (OT)

Gen.	Genesis	Ruth	Ruth
Exod.	Exodus	1 Sam.	1 Samuel
Lev.	Leviticus	2 Sam.	2 Samuel
Num.	Numbers	1 Kings	1 Kings
Deut.	Deuteronomy	2 Kings	2 Kings
Josh.	Joshua	1 Chron.	1 Chronicles
Judg.	Judges	2 Chron.	2 Chronicles

Ezra	Ezra	Dan.	Daniel
Neh.	Nehemiah	Hos.	Hosea
Esther	Esther	Joel	Joel
Job	Job	Amos	Amos
Ps.	Psalms	Obad.	Obadiah
Prov.	Proverbs	Jonah	Jonah
Eccl.	Ecclesiastes	Micah	Micah
Song. Sol.	Song of Solomon	Nahum	Nahum
(also Cant.)	(also Canticles)	Hab.	Habakkuk
Isa.	Isaiah	Zeph.	Zephaniah
Jer.	Jeremiah	Haggai	Haggai
Lam.	Lamentations	Zech.	Zechariah
Ezek.	Ezekiel	Mal.	Malachi

Selected Apocryphal and Deuterocanonical Works

1 Esdras	1 Esdras	Baruch	Baruch
2 Esdras	2 Esdras	Song 3	Song of the Three
Tobit	Tobit	Childr.	Children
Judith	Judith	Susanna	Susanna
Esther	Esther	Bel and Dr.	Bel and the
(Apocr.)	(Apocrypha)		Dragon
Wisd. of Sol.	Wisdom of	Prayer	Prayer of
(also Wisd.)	Solomon	Manasseh	Manasseh
	(also Wisdom)	1 Macc.	1 Maccabees
Ecclus.	Ecclesiasticus	2 Macc.	2 Maccabees
(also Sir.)	(also Sirach)		

New Testament (NT)

Matt.	Matthew	1 Thess.	1 Thessalonians
Mark	Mark	2 Thess.	2 Thessalonians
Luke	Luke	1 Tim.	1 Timothy
John	John	2 Tim.	2 Timothy
Acts	Acts	Tit.	Titus
Rom.	Romans	Philem.	Philemon
1 Cor.	1 Corinthians	Heb.	Hebrews
2 Cor.	2 Corinthians	Jas.	James
Gal.	Galatians	1 Pet.	1 Peter
Eph.	Ephesians	2 Pet.	2 Peter
Phil.	Philippians	1 John	1 John
Col.	Colossians	2 John	2 John

3 John	3 John	Rev. (also	Revelation (also
Jude	Jude	Apoc.)	Apocalypse)

Selected Apocryphal Works

G. Thom.	Gospel of Thomas	G. Pet.	Gospel of Peter
G. Heb.	Gospel of the Hebrews		

b. Shakespeare.

Ado	Much Ado about Nothing	MND	A Midsummer Night's Dream
Ant.	Antony and Cleopatra	MV	The Merchant of Venice
AWW	All's Well That Ends Well	Oth.	Othello
AYL	As You Like It	Per.	Pericles
Cor.	Coriolanus	PhT	The Phoenix and the Turtle
Cym.	Cymbeline	PP	The Passionate Pilgrim
Err.	The Comedy of Errors	Q	Quarto ed.
F1	First Folio ed. (1623)	R2	Richard II
F2	Second Folio ed. (1632)	R3	Richard III
Ham.	Hamlet	Rom.	Romeo and Juliet
1H4	Henry IV, Part I	Shr.	The Taming of the Shrew
2H4	Henry IV, Part II	Son.	Sonnets
H5	Henry V	TGV	The Two Gentlemen of Verona
1H6	Henry VI, Part I	Tim.	Timon of Athens
2H6	Henry VI, Part II	Tit.	Titus Andronicus
3H6	Henry VI, Part III	Tmp.	The Tempest
H8	Henry VIII	TN	Twelfth Night
JC	Julius Caesar	TNK	The Two Noble Kinsmen
Jn.	King John	Tro.	Troilus and Cressida
LC	A Lover's Complaint	Ven.	Venus and Adonis
LLL	Love's Labour's Lost	Wiv.	The Merry Wives of Windsor
Lr.	King Lear	WT	The Winter's Tale
Luc.	The Rape of Lucrece		
Mac.	Macbeth		
MM	Measure for Measure		

50 SYMBOLS AND ABBREVIATIONS USED IN PROOFREADING AND CORRECTION

a. Selected proofreading symbols. The symbols below are used in proofreading matter set in type. Many instructors use these symbols in correcting student papers.

᾿	Apostrophe or single quotation mark
‿	Close up (bask͡et ball)
᾿	Comma
ℐ	Delete
∧	Insert
¶	Begin a new paragraph
No ¶	Do not begin a new paragraph
⊙	Period
❝ ❞	Double quotation marks
#	Space
∼	Transpose elements, usually with "tr" in margin (th͡ier)

b. Common correction symbols and abbreviations.

Ab	Faulty abbreviation
Adj	Improper use of adjective
Adv	Improper use of adverb
Agr	Faulty agreement
Amb	Ambiguous
Awk	Awkward expression or construction
Cap	Faulty capitalization
D	Faulty diction
Dgl	Dangling construction
Frag	Fragment
lc	Use lower case
Num	Error in use of numbers
‖	Lack of parallelism
P	Faulty punctuation
Ref	Unclear pronoun reference
Rep	Unnecessary repetition
R-O	Run-on
Sp	Error in spelling

SS	Faulty sentence structure
T	Wrong tense of verb
Tr	Transpose elements
V	Wrong verb form
Wdy	Wordy

APPENDIX: PREPARATION OF THESES AND DISSERTATIONS

The following sections deal only with questions related specifically to the preparation of theses and dissertations. Information common to the research paper and the thesis or dissertation can be found in the appropriate sections above.

A SELECTION OF A THESIS TOPIC

Because a thesis or dissertation often takes months or years to complete, it is important to choose a topic that you can work with for a considerable period of time. Representing a new departure in either subject or method, the thesis or dissertation ought to make a substantial contribution to your field. Preliminary discussions with instructors, especially the thesis adviser, are invaluable in selecting a topic. Before the topic is presented for formal approval, all relevant sources—card catalog, bibliographies in the field, past volumes of *DA* and *DAI*, the *Comprehensive Dissertation Index*, and sources on foreign dissertations—should be consulted to verify the originality of the topic and to identify previous studies in the area. This step helps not only to modify and redefine the topic but also to provide the basic bibliography of the thesis. The thesis adviser and readers should be consulted for assistance in defining objectives, setting the limits of research, testing the soundness of arguments and conclusions, and improving the bibliography.

B THESIS PROSPECTUS OR OUTLINE

An important stage between the selection and approval of the thesis topic and the writing of the thesis is the presentation of the thesis prospectus or outline to the adviser. The thesis outline (following the basic arrangement given in Sec. 7) or the prospectus—usually accompanied by a preliminary bibliography—should be detailed. Often the prospectus or outline must receive the approval of the thesis adviser, the thesis committee, the entire department, and the dean of the graduate school as well.

C DIVISIONS OF THE TEXT

Unlike term papers (see Sec. 22), theses and dissertations have the formal divisions of a book:

Abstract
Title page
Copyright page
Dedication (optional)
Epigraph (optional)
Table of Contents
List of Illustrations (if applicable)
List of Tables (if applicable)
Preface
Acknowledgments (often combined with Preface)
Text
Appendix (if applicable)
Notes (if endnotes are permitted)
Glossary (if applicable)
Bibliography
Index (if applicable)

(Sometimes the thesis writer is required to include a curriculum vitae.) For recommendations regarding divisions within a chapter, see Sec. 22.

D PAGINATION

The preliminary material of the thesis or dissertation—including title page, copyright page, dedication, epigraph, table of contents, preface, and acknowledgments—should be assigned lowercase Roman numerals. Use Arabic numerals for paginating the text, appendix, endnotes, glossary, bibliography, and index. Although all pages, beginning with the title page, are counted in the total enumeration of the work, it is common practice not to place a number on the title page, the copyright page, the dedication, the epigraph, the first page of a chapter, or the first page of the following divisions: table of contents, list of illustrations, list of tables, preface, acknowledgments, appendix, endnotes, glossary, bibliography, and index.

E SPECIAL REQUIREMENTS FOR THESES AND DISSERTATIONS

Modern scholarship considers theses and dissertations as forms of publication in themselves, a view reinforced by the widespread practice of microfilm publication of dissertations. The pages of theses and dissertations should therefore resemble as closely as possible those of a printed book.

Unlike a term paper, the thesis or dissertation is always given a formal title page. The title page of the thesis usually includes title, author, thesis adviser, a statement indicating that the work has been submitted in partial fulfillment of degree requirements, and the date. The title of the thesis or dissertation, like that of the term paper, is not underlined, put in quotation marks, or capitalized in full; only published works, foreign words, and words cited in a linguistic study are underlined (see Sec. 21). Since requirements for the exact format of the title page vary from school to school, consult the department or graduate office.

Double-space the text of the dissertation, but, unless otherwise instructed, single-space all passages of verse and prose that are set off from the text (see Sec. 14) and all notes and citations in a bibliography. Skip a line between the notes to allow for raising the note number slightly (a half line, if the typewriter permits) and between citations in a bibliography.

Dissertations should be free of typing errors and bound in accordance with departmental or graduate school regulations. Leave margins of one inch at the top, bottom, and right side, but two inches on the left side to allow for binding. Type chapter titles two inches from the top of the page.

Since most dissertations are now microfilmed, a department or school may require the use of special thesis paper with preprinted margins. The department or graduate office also usually furnishes information on the acquisition of a copyright for the dissertation, the publication of an abstract (six hundred words or fewer) of the dissertation in *DAI,* and the microfilming of the work by University Microfilms International (300 North Zeeb Road, Ann Arbor, Michigan 48106).

F PERMISSIONS

In quoting in a work intended for publication—a thesis or dissertation but *not* a term paper—the writer must be fully aware of copyright law and the need to obtain permission to reproduce material from some sources. The copyright period in the United States currently extends to fifty years after the death of the author. After that date, the work enters the public domain; no longer protected by copyright, it is subject to appropriation by anyone without permission, but with proper attribution. (On plagiarism, see Sec. 6.) Until that time, however, a published book is protected by law. Although holders of a copyright may legally charge a fee for the reproduction of copyrighted material, especially if it is to be reproduced in a work undertaken in reasonable expectation of profit, United States copyright law states that a "fair use" of a copyrighted work for the purposes of "criticism, comment, news reporting, teaching . . . , scholarship, or research" is not an infringement of copyright. In practice, however, publishers differ widely on what constitutes "fair use." Many require permissions for short quotations, particularly of modern poetry, or for matter that is substantive (e.g., an apothegm). Both the *quantitative* and the *qualitative* nature of the quotation are important.

Fifty-three members of the Association of American University Presses have adopted a "Resolution on Permissions" that allows "scholars to quote without prior permission from published sources whatever they legitimately need to make their scholarly writings complete, accurate, and authenticated":

We the undersigned members of the Association of American University Presses agree as follows:
1. That publications issued under our imprints may be quoted without specific prior permission in works of original scholarship for accurate citation of authority or for criticism, review, or evaluation, subject to the conditions listed below.
2. That appropriate credit be given in the case of each quotation.
3. That waiver of the requirement for specific permission does not extend to quotations that are complete units in themselves (as poems,

letters, short stories, essays, journal articles, complete chapters or sections of books, maps, charts, graphs, tables, drawings or other illustrative materials), in whatever form they may be reproduced; nor does the waiver extend to quotation of whatever length presented as primary material for its own sake (as in anthologies or books of readings).

4. That the fact that specific permission for quoting materials may be waived under this agreement does not relieve the quoting author and publisher from the responsibility of determining "fair use" of such material.

Sixty-eight journals in the humanities have subscribed to a similar statement. Whenever seriously in doubt, consult the thesis adviser about whether a publisher or writer (depending upon who holds the copyright) should be asked for permission to quote. Permission is always required to quote from unpublished matter (such as letters and diaries) regardless of the age. When requesting permission to quote (or to reprint articles or sections of books), identify the material involved fully and accurately and specify the intended use (method of publication, publisher, intended audience, size of edition, etc.). Permissions in a dissertation should be credited on the copyright page or with the acknowledgments.

INDEX

References below are to numbered sections (e.g., 16c), not to pages. The first number in a reference often indicates a definition or general discussion of the subject.

Index

Index

Index

Index

individuals in series, numbers of 11e
Indonesian, transliteration of 17c
infinitives, capitalization of 15a
information services, documents of
  in bibliographies 44k
  in notes 35k
infra 48
insertions in research papers 25
inst. 48, 46
institutions, abbreviations of 46
instructor's name on research papers 21
instrumental music, titles of 13a
interlibrary loans 3, 4
interpolations 14e
  in quotations 10n, 14a, 14e
interviews
  in bibliographies 44j
  in notes 35j
introd. 48
introductions
  in bibliographies 42l
  in notes 31b, 32l
ips 48
issue numbers of periodicals
  in bibliographies 43c
  in notes 33e, 34c
  omission of 33e
It. 48
Italian
  capitalization in 15d
  names 16g
  titles 15d
italics 10h, 10k, 47 *See also* underlining

jacket notes of recordings
  in bibliographies 44h
  in notes 35h
Japanese
  names 16i
  transliteration of 17b
jour. 48, 46
journals *See also* periodicals
  indexes to popular journals 3
  titles of: English 15a, French 15b,
    German 15c, Italian 15d, Latin 15g,
    Portuguese 15e, Spanish 15f

Koran 13d
Korean
  names 16i
  transliteration of 17a

l., ll. 48, 15a
L 48
labels for illustrations 23

lang., langs. 48
languages
  abbreviations for 46
  indexes to research in modern
    languages 3
Lat. 48 *under* L
Latin
  capitalization in 15g
  reference words 47
  titles 15g
law cases *See* legal references
laws *See* legal references
L. C. 48, 46
lectures
  in bibliographies 44b
  in notes 35b
  titles of: 13b, English 15a, French 15b,
    German 15c, Italian 15d, Latin 15g,
    Portuguese 15e, Spanish 15f
legal references
  in bibliographies 42s
  in notes 32s
letters (of alphabet)
  lowercase, for notes to illustrations 23
  underlining 10h
letters to editor
  in bibliographies 43j
  in notes 34j
letters, personal
  in bibliographies 44i
  in notes 35i
libraries, using 3
  interlibrary loans 4
Library of Congress system 3
librettos
  in bibliographies 44h
  in notes 35h
ligatures 12e
line drawings 23
liner notes of recordings *See*
  jacket notes of recordings
linguistic examples 10h
linguistics, style manual of 39
list of illustrations in dissertations 23,
  App. C
list of tables in dissertations 23, App. C
literature, indexes to research in 3
ll. *See* l., ll.
loc. cit. 48, 37a

m. 48 *under* d.
M. 16e
M.A. 48
macrons in Japanese 17b
mag. 48, 46

147

Index

Index

Index

Index

sculpture
  in bibliographies 44f
  in notes 35f
  titles of 13a
s.d. 48 *under* n.d.
S. Doc. 48, 32r
seasons of periodicals, citing 33e, 33f
sec., secs. 48
sect., sects. 48 *under* sec.
sections *See also* divisions of text
  headings of 22
  of legal references 32s
  of newspapers 33g
  numbers of 22
semicolons 10l, 36
sentences
  omissions from 14d
  punctuation of 10
  structure of 9
ser. 48
series
  books: in bibliographies 42j; in notes
    31f, 32j
  periodicals: in bibliographies 43d; in
    notes 33d, 34d
  radio and television programs: in
    bibliographies 44g, in notes 35g
  titles of: 13d, English 15a, French 15b,
    German 15c, Italian 15d, Latin 15g,
    Portuguese 15e, Spanish 15f
sess. 48, 32r
set-down quotations *See* quotations, set
  off from the text
s.f. 48 *under* n.d.
Shakespeare, abbreviations for works of
  49b
ships, names of 13a
short novels
  in bibliographies 42h
  in notes 32h
short stories
  in bibliographies 42h
  in notes 32h
  titles of 13b
shortened forms in notes 31c, 31h, 37
sic 48
  in interpolations 14e
sig., sigs. 48, 15a, 31j, 32v
signatures
  in bibliographies 42v
  in notes 31j, 32v
single quotation marks 10k
  in quotations 14f
  in titles within titles 13c

single-spacing
  of footnotes 30
  in theses and dissertations App. E
s.l. 48 *under* n.p.
slashes 10m
  in dates 11c
  with note numbers 29
  in quotations of poetry 14b
soc. 48, 46
social sciences, index to research in 3
societies, names of 13d
sociology, abstracts of research in 3
songs, titles of 13b
sources *See also* documentation
  acknowledgment of 28
  of illustrations 23
  indirect: in bibliographies 44l, in notes
    35l
  of information: keeping a record in
    research 4, proper use of 6
  original not available 35l
  primary 40c
  of reprinted works: in bibliographies
    42h, in notes 32h
  secondary 40c
  of tables 23
Southeast-Asian languages,
  transliteration of 17c
Sp. 48
spacing 19 *See also* margins
  of abbreviations 46
  of bibliographical entries 41e
  of bibliography 40b
  following a colon 10c
  of dissertation App. E
  of divisions of text 22
  of illustrations 23
  within and between notes 30
  of periods in ellipsis 14d
  of quotations of poetry 14b
  of quotations of prose 14c
  of titles of papers 20, 21
Spanish
  capitalization in 15f
  names 16h
  titles 15f
special collections, use in research 3
speeches *See* lectures
spelling 12
  accents 12c
  British 9
  dieresis 12d
  modernization of 14a
  in quotations 14a

SAMPLE PAGES OF
A RESEARCH PAPER

Sample Pages

FIRST PAGE OF RESEARCH PAPER

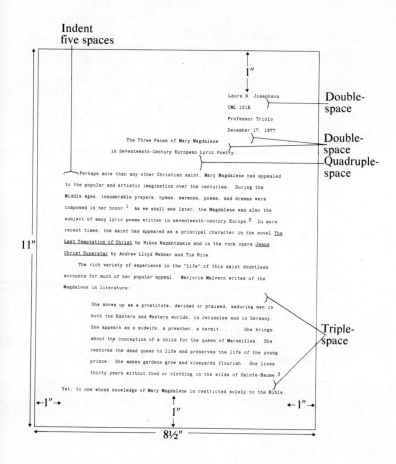

Indent five spaces

1"

Laura N. Josephson

CML 121E

Professor Triolo

December 17, 1977

The Three Faces of Mary Magdalene
in Seventeenth-Century European Lyric Poetry

Double-space

Double-space

Quadruple-space

Perhaps more than any other Christian saint, Mary Magdalene has appealed
to the popular and artistic imagination over the centuries. During the
Middle Ages, innumerable prayers, hymns, sermons, poems, and dramas were
composed in her honor.[1] As we shall see later, the Magdalene was also the
subject of many lyric poems written in seventeenth-century Europe.[2] In more
recent times, the saint has appeared as a principal character in the novel The
Last Temptation of Christ by Nikos Kazantzakis and in the rock opera Jesus
Christ Superstar by Andrew Lloyd Webber and Tim Rice.

The rich variety of experience in the "life" of this saint doubtless
accounts for much of her popular appeal. Marjorie Malvern writes of the
Magdalene in literature:

She shows up as a prostitute, derided or praised, seducing men in
both the Eastern and Western worlds, in Jerusalem and in Germany.
She appears as a midwife, a preacher, a hermit. . . . She brings
about the conception of a child for the queen of Marseilles. She
restores the dead queen to life and preserves the life of the young
prince. She makes gardens grow and vineyards flourish. She lives
thirty years without food or clothing in the wilds of Sainte-Baume.[3]

Triple-space

Yet, to one whose knowledge of Mary Magdalene is restricted solely to the Bible,

11"

←1"→   1"   ←1"→

8½"

Sample Pages

FIRST PAGE OF ENDNOTES

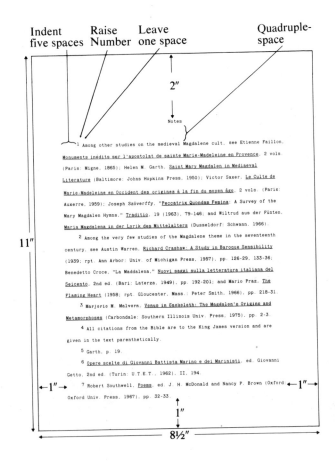

Indent
five spaces

Raise
Number

Leave
one space

Quadruple-
space

2″

Notes

11″

¹ Among other studies on the medieval Magdalene cult, see Etienne Faillon, Monuments inédits sur l'apostolat de sainte Marie-Madeleine en Provence, 2 vols. (Paris: Migne, 1865); Helen M. Garth, Saint Mary Magdalen in Mediaeval Literature (Baltimore: Johns Hopkins Press, 1950); Victor Saxer, Le Culte de Marie-Madeleine en Occident des origines à la fin du moyen âge, 2 vols. (Paris: Auxerre, 1959); Joseph Szövérffy, "Peccatrix Quondam Femina: A Survey of the Mary Magdalen Hymns," Traditio, 19 (1963), 79-146; and Wiltrud aus der Fünten, Maria Magdalena in der Lyrik des Mittelalters (Dusseldorf: Schwann, 1966).

² Among the very few studies of the Magdalene theme in the seventeenth century, see Austin Warren, Richard Crashaw: A Study in Baroque Sensibility (1939; rpt. Ann Arbor: Univ. of Michigan Press, 1957), pp. 126-29, 133-36; Benedetto Croce, "La Maddalena," Nuovi saggi sulla letteratura italiana del Seicento, 2nd ed. (Bari: Laterza, 1949), pp. 192-201; and Mario Praz, The Flaming Heart (1958; rpt. Gloucester, Mass.: Peter Smith, 1966), pp. 218-31.

³ Marjorie M. Malvern, Venus in Sackcloth: The Magdalen's Origins and Metamorphoses (Carbondale: Southern Illinois Univ. Press, 1975), pp. 2-3.

⁴ All citations from the Bible are to the King James version and are given in the text parenthetically.

⁵ Garth, p. 19.

⁶ Opere scelte di Giovanni Battista Marino e dei Marinisti, ed. Giovanni Getto, 2nd ed. (Turin: U.T.E.T., 1962), II, 194.

⁷ Robert Southwell, Poems, ed. J. H. McDonald and Nancy P. Brown (Oxford: Oxford Univ. Press, 1967), pp. 32-33.

←1″→

←1″→

1″

8½″

FIRST PAGE OF BIBLIOGRAPHY

Indent
five spaces

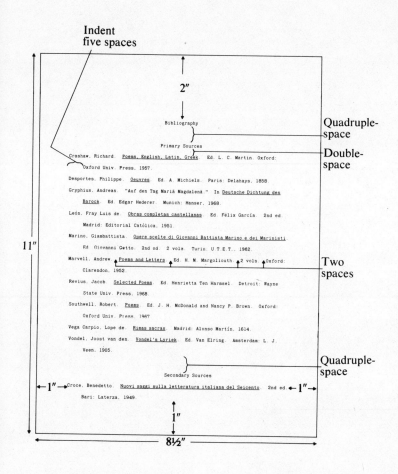

2"

Bibliography

Quadruple-
space

Primary Sources

Double-
space

Crashaw, Richard. <u>Poems, English, Latin, Greek</u>. Ed. L. C. Martin. Oxford:
Oxford Univ. Press, 1957.

Desportes, Philippe. <u>Oeuvres</u>. Ed. A. Michiels. Paris: Delahays, 1858.

Gryphius, Andreas. "Auf den Tag Mariä Magdalenä." In <u>Deutsche Dichtung des</u>
<u>Barock</u>. Ed. Edgar Hederer. Munich: Hanser, 1968.

León, Fray Luis de. <u>Obras completas castellanas</u>. Ed. Félix García. 2nd ed.
Madrid: Editorial Católica, 1951.

Marino, Giambattista. <u>Opere scelte di Giovanni Battista Marino e dei Marinisti</u>.
Ed. Giovanni Getto. 2nd ed. 2 vols. Turin: U.T.E.T., 1982.

Marvell, Andrew. <u>Poems and Letters</u>. Ed. H. M. Margoliouth. 2 vols. Oxford:
Clarendon, 1952.

Two
spaces

Revius, Jacob. <u>Selected Poems</u>. Ed. Henrietta Ten Harmsel. Detroit: Wayne
State Univ. Press, 1968.

Southwell, Robert. <u>Poems</u>. Ed. J. H. McDonald and Nancy P. Brown. Oxford:
Oxford Univ. Press, 1967.

Vega Carpio, Lope de. <u>Rimas sacras</u>. Madrid: Alonso Martín, 1614.

Vondel, Joost van den. <u>Vondel's Lyriek</u>. Ed. Van Elring. Amsterdam: L. J.
Veen, 1905.

Secondary Sources

Quadruple-
space

Croce, Benedetto. <u>Nuovi saggi sulla letteratura italiana del Seicento</u>. 2nd ed.
Bari: Laterza, 1949.

1"

1"

1"

11"

8½"